THE
STEAMBOAT
BERTRAND

The Bertrand during excavation, summer of 1969. (Photo © 1971, National Geographic Society.)

Publications in Archeology 11

THE STEAMBOAT BERTRAND

History, Excavation, and Architecture

by Jerome E. Petsche

National Park Service
U. S. Department of the Interior

Washington 1974

As the Nation's principal conservation agency, the Department of the Interior has basic responsibilities for water, fish, wildlife, mineral, land, park, and recreational resources. Indian and Territorial affairs are other major concerns of America's "Department of Natural Resources." The Department works to assure the wisest choice in managing all our resources so each will make its full contribution to a better United States—now and in the future.

This publication is the result of a study of an archeological and historic site on Federal land for which the National Park Service has had responsibilities. It is printed at the Government Printing Office, and may be purchased from the Superintendent of Documents, Washington, D. C. 20402.

Library of Congress Cataloging in Publication Data

Petsche, Jerome E
    The steamboat Bertrand.

    (Publications in archeology, 11)
    Bibliography: p. 165-170,
    Supt. of Docs. no.: I 29.59:11
    1. Bertrand (Steamboat) 2. Shipwrecks—
Missouri River. I. Title. II. Series.
E51.U75 no. 11   [VM461.5.B47]   913'.031'08s   [917.82'2]
                                                          72-600352

Publications in Archeology*

Archeological Research Series
1. Archeology of the Bynum Mounds, Mississippi (PB 177 061)**
2. Archeological Excavations in Mesa Verde National Park, Colorado, 1950 (PB 177 062)**
3. Archeology of the Funeral Mound, Ocmulgee National Monument, Georgia (PB 177 063)**
4. Archeological Excavations at Jamestown, Virginia (PB 177 064)**
5. The Hubbard Site and other Tri-wall Structures in New Mexico and Colorado
6. Search for the Cittie of Ralegh, Archeological Excavations at Fort Raleigh National Historic Site, North Carolina
7A. The Archeological Survey of Wetherill Mesa, Mesa Verde National Park, Colorado (Wetherill Mesa Studies)
7B. Environment of Mesa Verde, Colorado (Wetherill Mesa Studies)
7C. Big Juniper House, Mesa Verde National Park, Colorado (Wetherill Mesa Studies)
7D. Mug House, Mesa Verde National Park, Colorado (Wetherill Mesa Studies)
8. Excavations in the 17th-Century Jumano Pueblo, Gran Quivira, New Mexico
9. Excavations at Tse-ta'a, Canyon de Chelly National Monument, Arizona

Publications in Archeology
10. Ruins Stabilization in the Southwestern United States
11. The Steamboat Bertrand: History, Excavation, and Architecture

Anthropological Papers
1. An Introduction to Middle Missouri Archeology
2. Like-a-Fishhook Village and Fort Berthold, Garrison Reservoir, North Dakota

---

*Concurrent with the establishment of the Office of Professional Publications, National Park Service, the name of the *Archeological Research Series* has been changed to *Publications in Archeology*. The numbering of the volumes will not change. The series entitled *Anthropological Papers* is discontinued.

**These publications are no longer available from the Superintendent of Documents. They may be ordered by title (and parenthetical code number) by writing to: Clearinghouse, U.S. Department of Commerce, Springfield, Virginia, 22151. These reports are available in two forms: microfiche at 95 cents per document, or paper copy at $6.00 per volume, prepaid.

Figure 1. The hulk of the *Bertrand* with two-thirds of the cargo removed; view to the south. The decking, with the exception of a small portion amidships, starboard side, is removed. Note the surrounding well point system and depth of the stern to grassy surface in upper left-hand corner of photograph (*ca.* 30 feet). Early salvaging activity can be seen in the extreme bow where the forecastle was chopped and torn away. (Photo courtesy of *Woodman of the World Magazine*, Omaha, Nebraska.)

FOREWORD

This work is the result of a cooperative effort by two agencies of the U.S. Department of the Interior, the National Park Service and the Bureau of Sport Fisheries and Wildlife. It deals with the archeological excavation of the *Bertrand,* a mid-19th century riverboat discovered near the Missouri River on the DeSoto National Wildlife Refuge.

This important historic site was found on Federal land in 1968 by two private citizens, Messrs. Jesse Pursell and Sam Corbino of Omaha, and was excavated under the direction of National Park Service archeologists. The remains of the steamboat and its cargo fall under the broad protective purview of the 1906 Act for the Preservation of American Antiquities, and subsequent legislation. As custodian of the boat and its cargo, the Bureau of Sport Fisheries and Wildlife makes a significant contribution in protecting one of the Nation's most outstanding historic properties.

Rogers C.B. Morton
Secretary of the Interior

PREFACE

Late one cold afternoon in February, 1968, two men from Omaha, in search of treasure that had eluded many others for over a century, came close to realizing their dreams. Jesse Pursell and Sam Corbino had found the remains of the riverboat *Bertrand*, the sunken steamer that was a legend in many Iowa and Nebraska communities along the Missouri River. For as long as the oldest residents could remember, stories were told of the gold, whiskey, and mercury that awaited those fortunate enough to find the boat that had gone down in 1865 while enroute to Fort Benton, Montana Territory. But as is the case with so many dreams and visions of wealth, other men long ago had salvaged the *Bertrand* and had taken all but nine containers of mercury. The gold and kegs of whiskey reported to have been on board were never found during the 1968-69 excavations.

But the real treasure—that of the riverboat and the cargo in its holds—has become a part of the heritage of the people of the United States, to be displayed and protected for us by the Bureau of Sport Fisheries and Wildlife at the DeSoto National Wildlife Refuge. Always important as a resting and feeding place for hundreds of thousands of our nation's migrating wildfowl, the Refuge has become particularly significant now as one of those sites where American history will be made more meaningful and vivid for many future generations.

The remains of very few historic sites in the United States can compare with the diversity and number of cultural objects recovered from the riverboat's holds. Over three years were required to preserve and stabilize the goods meant to be used by our forebears a century ago. During those three years, scarcely a day passed at the laboratories of the DeSoto National Wildlife Refuge or of the Midwest Archeological Center of the National Park Service in Lincoln, Nebraska without the opening of a Bertrand shipping case, and the identification and preservation of still another historic tool or other product used in Montana Territory in the 1860's.

The remains of a sunken riverboat are valuable for the interpretation of an earlier way of life because of the accidental nature of their loss, their undisturbed preservation, and their intrinsic interest. Catastrophes arising from volcanic eruptions, storms at sea, and tur-

bulent rivers often result in instant preservation of significant archeological evidence. The *Bertrand* is an excellent example of this kind of
preservation.

As will become clear to those who read Mr. Petsche's book,
the *Bertrand* is not simply a unique historic site investigated by a few
persons for the edification of a small number of archeologists and historians. It is one for which many persons gave of their talents, and
one for which two agencies of the Federal Government—the Bureau
of Sport Fisheries and Wildlife, and the National Park Service—mar-
shalled their forces. And it is one for which two determined private
citizens, Messrs. Pursell and Corbino, exercised extraordinary skill in
locating the sunken riverboat and then cooperated with Federal authorities to excavate and thus initiate processes which would result in
the saving of one of America's most meaningful treasures of the past.

Ronald H. Walker, *Director*
National Park Service

ACKNOWLEDGMENTS

Hundreds of persons have had some association with the Bertrand project, ranging from the highest ranking administrators of the National Park Service and Bureau of Sport Fisheries and Wildlife in Washington, D.C., to young archeology students who gave up their summers to wield shovels and water hoses in some of the sloppiest and most intractable mud and clay the Missouri River is capable of producing.

To the salvors themselves, Jesse Pursell and Sam Corbino, must go the gratitude and appreciation of all those charged with the responsibility of the boat and its cargo as a historic site of national significance. Even when it became clear that their hopes of recovering the vast treasure trove once reported to have been on the *Bertrand* would never be realized, their good will, perseverance, and efforts to assist National Park Service (NPS) archeologists and officials of the Bureau of Sport Fisheries and Wildlife (BSFW) protect and preserve the remains were exemplary.

I owe a very personal debt of gratitude to Wilfred D. Logan, former Chief of the Midwest Archeological Center, Lincoln, Nebr., who was made responsible for the administration of the Bertrand project for the NPS. He and his assistant, Jackson W. Moore Jr., were involved from the very beginning of the search and excavation, and I relied many times upon their advice, counsel, and encouragement.

To the managers of the DeSoto National Wildlife Refuge during the period of excavation, Kermit Dybsetter, James Salyer, and Assistant Manager Wayne Chord, go my thanks for assistance I cannot begin to detail here. In addition to their problems of administering the entire Refuge and the safekeeping of Bertrand artifacts with a small staff, their concern for and interest in my particular problems never once flagged.

Unique as an archeological experience, necessitating the employment of recovery and preservation techniques used by those who work both under water and on dry land sites, and the need to innovate nearly every day, the Bertrand project challenged the talents of many authorities. The outstanding contributions of Professor Frank Hengeveld, chairman of the Department of Chemistry at Dana College, Blair, Nebr., and his daughter, Pamela, made possible the

viii

boatwood studies in Appendices C and D. Professor Hengeveld volunteered the use of his chemistry laboratory, including the analytical balances, Olivetti computer, and ovens. He and his daughter were of particular assistance in helping design the studies presented in the appendices which provide insights into the buoyancy and drying rates of Bertrand boatwood. These preliminary studies, made when the hull was still exposed, were initiated through the encouragement of Ray M. Seborg, Consultant in Wood Products, Forest Products Laboratory, U.S. Forest Service. Dr. Seborg's general assessment of the hull is presented in Appendix B, and was made following a personal inspection of the boat at the time most of it was exposed.

The assistance of several NPS staff archeologists in the Office of Archeology and Historic Preservation was most appreciated, that of George R. Fischer in particular. Mr. Fischer placed us in contact with a number of authorities on preservation, architecture, engineering, and steamboating. Furthermore, he spent several days with us in the mud and 100-degree temperatures at the Bertrand site.

The scale drawings of the remains of the *Bertrand* accompanying this report represent the work of a number of archeologists and their students, architects, and illustrators. To Jerry Livingston, Scientific Illustrator at the Midwest Archeological Center in Lincoln, Nebr., we are indebted for the rendering of final interpretive sketches and graphic reconstructions. His work, in consultation with the author, was based on many field photographs of the hull made during excavation; on historic photographs of riverboats similar to the *Bertrand*; the on-site scale drawings of the author and Mark Lancaster, architect, of Detroit, Mich.; the work of David Gradwohl, Associate Professor of Anthropology, Iowa State University, and his students; and the advice of several leading American authorities on the history of steamboating. These include Alan L. Bates, Louisville, Ky., Bert Fenn, Tell City, Ind., and Captain Frederick Way, Jr., Sewickley, Pa.

Mention must be made and appreciation noted of the unique talents of the preservators involved in the conservation of Bertrand artifacts. They include Carl M. Semczak of Detroit, Mich., and Barbara L. Daniels of Albuquerque, N.M., who set up the original emergency laboratory for processing artifacts at the Refuge, and Ronald R. Switzer who was in charge of the immense task of preserving the cargo at the laboratories on the Refuge and at the Midwest Archeological Center. Mr. Switzer contributed the synopsis on conservation of Bertrand artifacts in Appendix A, and is now preparing a manuscript on the preservation and conservation of historic materials recovered in fresh water—a work that should prove both exhaustive and of lasting value to all of us who work on the recovery, stabilization, and interpretation of historic materials.

Individuals who consulted with us and provided advice in the areas of history, preservation, pathology, engineering, illustration, and architecture, include Denys Peter Myers, Principal Architectural Historian, Historical American Buildings Survey, NPS; the Rev. Clifford M. Lewis, S.J., Assistant to the President of Wheeling College, Wheeling, W.Va.; Mendel L. Peterson, Director, Underwater Exploration Project, Nadja Makovenyi, Visual Information Specialist, and Robert M. Organ, Director, Conservation and Analytical Laboratory, all of the Museum of History and Technology, Smithsonian Institution; Rolland O. Hower, Office of Exhibits, Museum of Natural History, Smithsonian Institution; Terry L. Highly, Plant Pathologist, Forest Research Laboratory of the U.S. Forest Service; Col. Pierre A. Fink and George Migaki, both of the Armed Forces Institute of Pathology; James B. "Pat" Smith, Museum Specialist, Division of Museums, NPS; William J. Peterson, Superintendent, State Historical Society of Iowa; Marvin F. Kivett, Director, Nebraska State Historical Society; and Charles Martin, President, Greater Omaha Historical Society.

In addition to the above, I am indebted to the staffs of the state historical societies of Nebraska, Iowa, Missouri, Montana, and the Merchantile Archives of St. Louis, Mo., for photographs and access to archives.

I am especially grateful to Louis C. Hunter, retired chairman of the Department of History, American University, who read the manuscript. As the dean of all students of the western steamboat and authority on early American river transportation, his advice and criticism were most helpful.

In one way or another, nearly every employee of the DeSoto National Wildlife Refuge, BSFW, and of the Midwest Archeological Center, NPS, turned from their usual tasks to devote nearly full time to the Bertrand project. Some of the most physically taxing work was accomplished by volunteers, some of whom labored over two months, either in the emergency laboratory set up at the Refuge headquarters, or in the Bertrand excavation. The volunteers include Nancy Osborn, graduate student in anthropology at Iowa State University (later employed as a laboratory assistant); Jerome D. Alexander, retired Omaha businessman; Helene Bowditch, of Ripon, Wis.; Mrs. Susan Bodie Traub, of Lincoln, Nebr.; and John M. Logan, an undergraduate student, University of North Dakota.

Discovery of the *Bertrand* in 1968 came as a jolt and a challenge to nearly everyone associated with the crash project. Certain administrators of Federal agencies were doubly burdened at the time with their normal jobs and with the added responsibility of coordinating activities of the National Park Service and the Bureau of Sport

Fisheries and Wildlife. These remarkable contributions were made under pressure of time and involved planning, fiscal management, procurement, and transfer of employees associated with the project. Those primarily involved include Phillip S. Morgan, Assistant Regional Refuge Supervisor, BSFW; Charles C. Carothers III, Special Assistant to the Assistant Secretary of the Interior for Fish and Wildlife, Parks and Marine Resources; Llynn A. Greenwalt, Associate Regional Refuge Director, BSFW; H. Jesse Grove, Interpretive Specialist, BSFW; Ed Crozier, Joe Knecht, Charles Johnston, and Elaine Rhode, National Planning Team, BSFW; Warren W. Wisby, Director, National Aquarium, BSFW; Ernest A. Connally, Associate Director for Professional Services, NPS; John M. Corbett, former Chief, and Zorro A. Bradley, former Assistant Chief, Division of Anthropology and Archeology, NPS; and J.E.N. (Joe) Jensen, Assistant Director, NPS, Service Center Operations.

And, finally, something must be said of the extraordinary work of James Stolz, a graduate student in wildlife management from Purdue University. Jim came to work for the Refuge during the summer of 1969 through a special student program of BSFW, and was assigned to assist me in the excavation and research of the boat. This young Illinois farm boy and outstanding student excelled in everything he did, including the scale drawing of ship's parts, recording cargo, photography, mapping, maintaining equipment, historical research, and assisting in the wood studies. The only time I can remember his asking for time off was to watch the televised launching of Apollo 11 that carried the first men to the moon—the only adventure in Jim's opinion that could hold a candle to that of the *Bertrand*.

J.E.P.

November, 1972
Washington, D.C.

CONTENTS

ILLUSTRATIONS

Frontispiece. The Bertrand during excavation

Figure 2. Artist's interpretation of the *Bertrand* on the Missouri. This sketch and other renderings of the ship's lines and reconstructions are based on scale drawings and photographs of the remains of the boat made by archeologists and architects during excavation. Supplementary information on appearance of details was derived from early photographs and descriptions of riverboats of the same general class, of similar construction, and period of use.

GLOSSARY

A specialized vocabulary came into use by rivermen and boatwrights during the 80 years of steamboat development in the United States. Many of the terms are borrowings from the language of seamen and have undergone slight or substantial modifications in meaning. Others have been in use for centuries by carpenters and other artisans, but also take on different connotations when used in reference to riverboats.

Arm A paddlewheel spoke, one end of which is attached to a flange, and the other to the buckets (paddles).

Ash trough A long metal pan under the grates to catch ashes from the firebox; coursed with firebrick, and extending to the trapdoor on the guard.

Athwartship Across the ship from side to side.

Beam Breadth of vessel athwartship, measured from inside planking; also, a horizontal supporting member.

Bitts A pair of vertical posts supporting a horizontal timber in the bow; used in tying lines and similar in function to a kevel.

Boiler deck The deck immediately above the boilers; usually served as the base or floor of the cabin area on packets.

Break The point at which an upper deck ends and from which there is a drop to a deck on a lower level.

Buckets Planks extending from the arms of the paddle wheel and forming the paddles.

Bulkhead Any upright partition separating compartments or holds.

Bull rails Removable rails used on the main deck between the stationaries to facilitate loading.

Bustle Bulges in the stern rake; a result of building the stern in such a way that the forward portion of the balance rudders clear the stern rake with minimal space.

Buttocklines Contours on body plans where a vertical plane parallel to the centerline intersects the hull.

Cant To turn or angle from the horizontal.

xvii

Capstan Powered drum mounted on vertical axle; used with lines to move heavy objects or the boat itself.

Carlines Joists running athwartship supporting boiler and texas decks; *cf.* deck beams.

Carvel-built Planks of hull set flush at the seams; as opposed to clinker-built, *i.e.*, planks or strakes overlapping.

Chain plates Thick, wooden plates bolted to the side and bottom ribs or a keelson, and to which are connected the hog chains.

Chine The knuckle where the sides of the boat meet the bottom and form an angle.

Coaming Curbs around the edges of decks.

Cocked hat. A triangular wooden component used to brace paddle wheel arms, or as a wooden brace for hull framing.

Crank Metal arm connected to the pitman and paddle wheel shaft; that portion of the assembly which changes linear to circular motion.

Crown A slight lateral curve in the decks athwartship to facilitate drainage of rain water, or decks awash; also referred to as *the camber*.

Davit Crane of wood or metal for raising and lowering the dory or workboat.

Dead flat Transverse section of the vessel with the largest area, the ends from which sheer upwards in the bow and stern.

Deadwood *See skeg*.

Deck beams Joists running athwartship and to which the main decking is attached; *cf.* carlines.

Draft That portion of the hull extending into the water; traditionally measured vertically in feet when light (empty vessel) and/or heavy (fully loaded vessel).

False transom A vertical surface of the hull aft of the transom and rudders.

Forecastle The forward portion of the vessel, including superstructure, main decking and appurtenances.

Flanges Paddle wheel hubs attached to the shaft, and to which the arms are attached.

Grasshoppering A method of levering a vessel over sandbars or other shallow areas with a pair of spars and derrick rigged in the bow.

Guard A deck outboard of the hull on which cargo was carried and/or to provide a walkway; originally meant to protect the paddle wheel.

Hog To curve upward amidships, or downward at stern and stem; used in reference to the conformity of the hull when unbraced.

Hog chains Iron rods, varying in diameter from about 1½ to 2½ inches, used in the trussing system to support the bow and stern and, often, the sides of the hull.

Hog chain braces Wooden timbers supporting hog chains, projecting at various angles from keelsons or other major supporting members of the hull bottom; a part of the trussing system to prevent hogging.

Ice shield Iron sheeting outboard on the bow, extending above and below the waterline to protect the vessel from ice and other obstructions.

Keelson A major supporting structural member in the hull bottom parallel to vessel length.

Kevel A wooden or iron assembly fastened to the deck with ends projecting beyond the center, and to which lines may be belayed or fastened for tie-down of the vessel.

Mud drum Hollow cylinder under the boilers; used to collect sediment from the boilers.

Outriggers Horizontal wooden braces supporting the guards.

Pillow block Supporting members of a shaft bearing; a mounting for the paddle wheel bearing, countersunk into the aft extension of the cylinder timber.

Pitman Connecting rod between engine crosshead and the paddle wheel crank.

Quarter Extreme after part of a vessel's side.

Rake Inclination from a vertical or horizontal direction; usually in reference to turn of bilge in stern and bow.

Scantling Boards used for framing.

Scarf joint Method of joining side and bottom planking or strakes to increase sheer strength.

Sheave A roller chock attached to kevel to facilitate easy movement of lines and to reduce rope friction.

Sheer Longitudinal upward curve of the deck and lines of the vessel viewed from the side.

Skeg A fin ahead of the rudders to prevent side slip.

Spar chain straps A ring or chain on the outer bow sides, used as a guide and fulcrum for the spars employed in grasshoppering.

Stanchions Upright members supporting rails, decks, etc.

Stationaries Stanchions supporting the outboard edge of the boiler deck.

Steam drum Cylinder situated above the boilers; used to collect and hold steam for transmission to engines.

Stempiece Timber or iron rod running from the hull bottom and curving upward to the deck; the forward most component of the vessel.

Strake A breadth of planks, either bottom or sides of hull, forming a continuous strip from stem to stern; also used to refer to a single plank of the above assembly.

Texas deck The deck above the boiler deck on which a cabin (above the skylight roof) is attached.

Timberhead Wooden or metal posts used for tying lines in the bow.

Transom The aftermost of the square frames, or the vertical planks at the stern of the hull.

Yoke Heavy supporting beams in the bow of a vessel.

Figure 3. A small portion of the cargo removed from the *Bertrand* and stored prior to preservation in a cool, moist atmosphere. (Photo courtesy of American Telephone & Telegraph Co., Long Lines Department.)

PART **1**

INTRODUCTION

In late February of 1968, two Omaha salvors, Jesse Pursell and Sam Corbino, encountered evidence of a buried steamboat near the present channel of the Missouri River, approximately 25 miles upstream from Omaha on the DeSoto National Wildlife Refuge. The remains of the vessel lay below the water table in silt and clay at a mean depth of 28 feet from the surface (fig. 1). Drawing on information in old maps, early newspaper accounts, and abstracts of land ownership, supplemented by the use of a flux gate magnetometer, the salvors encountered the first physical evidence of the boat with a 6-inch auger drilled from ground surface through the hull bottom. The craft was subsequently identified during cargo removal as the *Bertrand*, principally on the basis of cursive lettering in stenciling ink on the side of a number of boxes which read "Bertrand Stores."

A steamer of the Upper Ohio class or type, the *Bertrand* was known to have sunk in DeSoto Bend on April 1, 1865. Enroute from St. Louis, Mo., to Fort Benton, Montana Territory, she carried a cargo of foodstuffs, clothing, agricultural and mining supplies, and, according to historic sources, a large amount of mercury for use in the amalgaming process of gold refining. The successful location and complete excavation of the cargo in 1968-69 thus ended periodic searches by others stretching back nearly a century.

The discovery also modified local tradition which held that the *Bertrand* contained fabulous wealth, not only in the form of mercury (some sources report 35,000 pounds), but also in the form of 5,000 gallons of whiskey in oaken casks—and even gold. The sum total of the treasure trove, however, was limited to mercury in nine containers. A good deal of evidence encountered in the excavation during the summer of 1969 is indicative of previous salvage attempts, and the small amount of mercury was recovered in a context that lead the author to the conclusion that the containers were simply overlooked in a previous salvage attempt.

In early 1968, the salvors sought and signed a contract[1] with

---

[1]Number GS-00-DP-(S)-80501 and dated January 3, 1968. As a result of the long period of time required to find the boat and complete excavation, the contract was subsequently amended (renewed) on March 11 and again on July 22, 1968, and January 13, 1969.

the General Services Administration, a prerequisite to a search and recovery of treasure trove on Federal land. According to conditions of the contract, the salvors, if successful, were to receive 60 percent of the value of the trove, specified as mercury, whiskey, and gold—the Federal Government to retain 40 percent. The contract further provided, in Article 2, that the salvors be "guided during any excavation by the advice of the Chief, Midwest Archeological Center, National Park Service." Furthermore, the contract was made subject to provisions of the Act for the Preservation of American Antiquities, approved June 8, 1906 (24 Stat. 225), and the implementing rules and regulations. Article 12 of the contract further states that "any artifacts (to include all man-made objects or parts thereof) or other valuable historical items that may be recovered, must remain the property of the United States Government and shall be given into the custody of the Refuge Manager."

From the outset of the search in 1967, administration of National Park Service responsibilities to assure compliance with the Antiquities Act fell to Wilfred D. Logan, Chief, Midwest Archeological Center. He was present at the Bertrand site at all times during excavation considered critical for the preservation of the sunken riverboat, and during the fall and early winter of 1968 when the first cargo was removed from the stern holds. The author was then assigned to initiate the research and supervise the excavation. He was present throughout the excavation period of 1969, and remained until the cargo was completely recovered, the well point system removed, and the water table again allowed to rise, leaving the hulk under 12 feet of water, silt and sand. Field notes, charts, maps, scale drawings, and photographs were made under the direction of the author from the time of initial exposure of the steamer to the backfilling operation. Authorities on preservation and stabilization, architects, and engineers were consulted from time to time, and, until more permanent facilities were installed, a temporary field laboratory was arranged at the headquarters of the refuge.

The historical significance of the vast amount of cargo may be considered in one respect as material culture "captured in time," precisely dated, and quite representative of the mining technology and frontier economy of mid-19th century North America. Such potential for the interpretation of American history was immediately recognized by the Secretary of the Interior's Advisory Board on National Parks, Historic Sites, Buildings and Monuments. A memorandum issued by the Board states, in part, that it "...regards the *Bertrand* and its contents as a type specimen, exceptionally valuable for study and illustrative purposes and, therefore, of national historical significance within the meaning of the Historic Sites Act of 1935." As comparative collections, that portion of the cargo which can normally be expected to survive longest in other historic sites (bottles, buttons, glass, hardware, etc.) should be of considerable importance to the archeologist and historian focusing attention on the upper Missouri.

No attempt will or could be made in this book to provide a detailed description of the *Bertrand's* contents. In Part IV a gross identification of the cargo is presented along with information relating to consignees and manufacturers—obtained chiefly through the field recording of labels and stenciling. Full descriptions, accession, and stabilization of the material will necessarily continue for years, providing rare opportunities for further study of frontier technology as well as the preservation of material exposed to a fresh water environment for over a century. Early estimates made during the summer excavation period of 1969 place the total volume of the cargo at just over 10,000 cubic feet. The material which has not already undergone stabilization is wrapped in polyethylene and is stored in a cool, moist atmosphere at the DeSoto National Wildlife Refuge. While individual artifacts may number somewhat short of 2 million, an estimated 300,000 items would appear to warrant stabilization and/or restoration for purposes of future study and museum exhibition. In addition to the foodstuffs, liquor, and patent medicines, these include objects of leather, wood, glass and porcelain, ceramics (stoneware, china, iron (wrought, drawn, cast), hard rubber, shell, textiles (wool, silk, cotton), ivory, bone, brass, copper, tin, lead, etc.

While it is anticipated that the material recovered will provide abundant data for future descriptive and analytical papers—not to speak of research directed to preservation—enough field and archival data have been assembled to present this study on the excavation and history of the boat. The purposes of this book, in the main, are fivefold: (1) to relate the history of the *Bertrand* with reference to steamboating on the Missouri and the frontier economy of Montana Territory during the mid-1860's; (2) to describe the techniques used in the search, location, and subsequent excavation of the riverboat; (3) to present a graphic reconstruction of the architecture and other descriptive information on the remains and physical condition of the craft; (4) to present a gross, descriptive account of the cargo and shipping data recorded in the field; and (5) to describe immediate, emergency procedures taken to insure optimum preservation of the cargo and boat under the prevailing circumstances and facilities of the DeSoto National Wildlife Refuge.

Figure 4. The *Bertrand* began its journey to the gold regions from this wharf at St. Louis in 1865. The photograph is believed to have been taken in 1867. (Photo courtesy of the Missouri Historical Society, St. Louis, Mo.)

NORTH EAST VIEW.

Figure 5. Granville Stuart's pen and ink rendering of Fort Benton in 1869, view to the northeast. Fort Benton, destination of the *Bertrand*, was the terminus for steamer transportation on the Missouri. Stuart was one of the major consignees of *Bertrand* cargo. (Photo of rendering, courtesy of the Montana Historical Society, Helena, Mont.)

PART 2

ORIGINS
AND
HISTORY

The *Bertrand* leaves today on her first trip for St. Louis; she has 6,000 kegs of nails and other freight, making a good load. She is a nice trim little steamer, neat but not gaudy, and sits upon the water like a duck. She has a hundred and sixty-two feet [sic] deck[1], draws when light about 18 inches...Her Captain, Ben Goodwin, is a well known river man, and Jerry Cochrane goes as Clerk. If the people down on the lower waters only knew Jerry as well as they do up here, they'd all want to travel on his boat—that's all. *Wheeling Daily Intelligencer*, Wheeling, West Virginia, November 26, 1864.

Scarcely five months after the item appeared in the newspaper of the *Bertrand's* port of berth, the steamer that was reported to have sat on the water like a duck lay swamped under the treacherous waters of the Missouri. How she came to be a part of the upper Missouri river traffic is not altogether certain, but it cannot be surprising in view of the economic conditions of the day. The need for "mountain" steamers at the time was pressing, and the entrepreneurs of river transportation in St. Louis were buying every low draft boat they could obtain. Headed for gold country, the *Bertrand* was enroute from St. Louis to Fort Benton, Montana Territory, with passengers and equipment for the mines and outposts of the frontier (fig. 6). On April 1, 1865 she struck a snag at a location that was then known as "Portage La Force" a few thousand yards below DeSoto Landing, approximately 25 river miles upstream from Omaha. Rumored to

---

[1]The *Bertrand* was officially enrolled as a 161-foot vessel (measured from the tip of the bow to the transom); Record Group 41, Records of the Bureau of Marine Inspection and Navigation, General Services Administration, National Archives and Record Service, Washington D.C. An earlier steamer on the Missouri, also named *Bertrand*, was licensed for the coasting trade by the Port of St. Louis for the years 1857-58; Bureau of Customs, Record Group 36, Federal Records Center, General Services Administration, Kansas City, Mo.

6

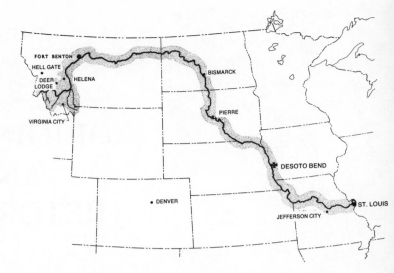

Figure 6. The intended route of the *Bertrand* in 1865, from St. Louis to Fort Benton, Montana Territory.

have been lost with a cargo of quicksilver, whiskey, and even gold, the story of her sinking became a legend of remarkable proportions. For a century she had been the object of many searches, and only until her remains were discovered in 1968 was the full impact of her role in early river traffic on the frontier appreciated.

CONSTRUCTION AND ENROLLMENT

Although early historical documentation is scarce, enough can be pieced together to present a reasonably accurate account of her construction, initial owners, and movements. According to the Wheeling newspaper account, the hull was fabricated in the yards of Dunlevy & Co.; the engines and machinery were built and installed by the Sweeney iron foundry;[2] the cabins were made by Gullet[3] of Pittsburgh, and the furnishings supplied by one Mendels (*Wheeling Daily Intelligencer*, November 26, 1864). The formal enrollment record lists her original owners as George Feller and Thomas H. Reed, both of Wheeling, W. Va., and George Laing, Lewis W. Cochran, and Jeremiah Cochran, of Monroe County, Ohio (Record Group 41, GSA, National Archives, Washington, D.C.).

[2]Wheeling records for the period list an A.J. Sweeney & Son as owning an iron works and boat building establishment. Personal communication, Clifford M. Lewis, S. J., Research Analyst, West Virginia Survey of Historic Places for the National Register, Wheeling College, W. Va.

[3]The Gullet mentioned in the news account may have been one Isaac Gullet, listed in Pittsburgh city directories from 1863 to 1874. He was a carpenter living in Allegheny City, now the north side of Pittsburgh.

Figure 7. John J. Roe of St. Louis, a part owner of the *Bertrand*. (Photo of steel engraving, courtesy of the Missouri Historical Society, St. Louis, Mo.)

The *Bertrand's* date of enrollment, November 25, 1864, would indicate that she was constructed some time in the summer of that year. Her tonnage was listed at 251, her length at 161 feet, beam 32 feet 9 inches, and mean depth of hold, 5 feet 2 inches (*ibid.*). Although there was a tendency on the part of owners during the mid-1800's to overstate capacity and understate tonnage to reduce fees and taxes, estimates for western riverboats at the time placed cargo capacity at one-third to one-half greater than the figures of measured tonnage (Hunter, 1949, p. 83).

Mention of only two original crew members appears in the early Wheeling newspaper account. Ben Goodwin, the steamer's master on the Wheeling to St. Louis run, was a pilot and captain on the Ohio and Mississippi rivers, and the Jerry Cochrane mentioned as clerk appears likely to have been the Jeremiah Cochran listed in the enrollment record as part owner (*Wheeling Daily Intelligencer*, November 26, 1864). As the active business manager of the boat and keeper of accounts, it was not uncommon for the clerk to own a share of the vessel.

Presumably, the maiden voyage of the *Bertrand* followed the route of other steamers constructed for the western trade in the Wheeling-Pittsburgh area, i.e., down the Ohio to its confluence with the Mississippi, then up the river to St. Louis. Approximately three and one-half months after her departure, advertisements appeared in St. Louis newspapers heralding her planned trip to gold mining regions of Montana Territory (*Daily Missouri Democrat*, March 10, 1865). At approximately this time, the vessel appears to have changed hands, and was now a part of the Montana and Idaho Transportation Line (*ibid.*). She thus joined the company's fleet of mountain steamers which included the *Benton, Yellowstone, Fanny Ogden,* and the *Deer Lodge*. The firm, at that time the most active and largest engaged in upper Missouri trade in the mid-1860's, was started during the winter of 1864-65 by John G. Copelin and John J. Roe (Lass, 1962, pp. 42, 43).

Roe, a former steamboat captain on the Ohio (fig.7) was a prominent St. Louis businessman with extensive capital and interests in insurance, banking, and transportation (Edwards and Hopewell 1860, p. 201). He and his son-in-law, Copelin, seem to have formed the company with the express purpose of offering through bills of lading for freight destined for the mining country in Montana Territory (*Daily Missouri Republican*, March 18, 1865). As organizers of a wagon freight line and owners of mountain steamers, the men appear to have attempted a transportation monoply.[4] And, in addition to their interests in transportation, Roe himself was engaged in a wholesaling and retailing establishment in Virginia City (*Montana Post*, October 8, 1864). In the process of excavating the *Bertrand's* cargo, it was noted that the name J. J. Roe appeared as a consignee in brushed stenciling ink on containers of foodstuffs and hardware sent from the east coast. It thus appears that as consignee of merchandise in St. Louis, and as river and wagon shippers of their own as well as others' goods, the Roe and Copelin combine appears to have been designed to corner a large part of the shipping and supply markets on the northwestern frontier.

DEPARTURE AND SINKING

By mid-March of 1865, preparations were being made by the Montana and Idaho Transportation Line to sign on a crew, secure passengers, and to load the freight. Typical of advertisements running as early as February 22, 1865, is the following from the *Tri-Weekly Missouri Democrat*:

> FORT BENTON PACKET, Idaho and the Gold Mines. The new, fast and light draught steamer BERTRAND, Ohlman, master, will leave St. Louis for Fort Benton on the opening of navigation to Omaha. Shippers and passengers seeking transportation to Fort Benton, Virginia City, Deer Lodge, and the Bitter Root Valley cannot fail to improve this opportunity.
>
> The steamer Bertrand is of light draught, with good carrying capacity and most excellent cabin accomodations, insuring to freighters and passengers that speed and safety so essential on a trip of this kind. Shippers may rely upon this being one of the first boats to Benton. For freight or passage apply to: Capt. Jas. A. Yore, Southwest Corner Chesnut and Main Streets. Boyde and Sylvestre, Agents; 74 Commercial Street.

Despite the mention of an Ohlman as master in the advertisement, the *Bertrand* left St. Louis on Saturday morning at 10 a.m.

---

[4]Overland freighting businesses at Ft. Benton in 1865 included J. J. Roe and Co.; Stuart, King and Gillette; Thomas Ryan and John G. Copelin; and Worden and Co. (*Montana Post*, April 1, 1865)

with James A. Yore as captain (*Daily Missouri Democrat*, March 17, 1865). One of a family of riverboat captains on the Missouri, Mississippi, and Ohio rivers, Yore is listed in several comtemporary newspaper accounts and one historical article as an owner of the vessel (McDonald, 1927, p. 229). Other accounts list ownership by "Copelin and Co. of St. Louis" (*Council Bluffs Non Pareil*, April 3, 1865), and the Montana and Idaho Transportation Line (*Daily Missouri Democrat*, March 10, 1865). And while it seems clear that the *Bertrand* was part of the mountain fleet of the latter company—the major stockholders of which were Roe and Copelin—Yore, as master, very likely had an interest in the boat.

Reports of the *Bertrand's* departure from the St. Louis levee are scanty, but following several delays, she seems to have left at 10 a.m., Saturday, March 18th (*Daily Missouri Democrat*, March 17, 1865). Rivermen, watching for the mid-March rise of the Missouri, were reporting a rising river and excellent conditions for the mountain run at this time and, in addition to the five packets of the Montana and Idaho Transportation Line, at least three other steamers were poised for their northern journey.[5] Approximately two weeks after her departure, news began filtering back to St. Louis and to Virginia City of the loss of the *Bertrand* and much of her cargo. Typical of Montana Territory newspaper reports is the following:

> STEAMBOAT SUNK—The Steamer Bertrand sunk above Omaha while on her voyage hither. The passengers among whom were Mrs. Atchison and Mrs. Millard, with their children are all safe and sound, but they have lost their baggage. The cargo was nearly all insured. We hear from Mr. R. Simpson that Gen. Dorris,[6] one of our pioneer merchants, lost a part of the goods he was bringing to this city. (*Montana Post*, April 22, 1865).

Information on the sinking of the *Bertrand* is limited, although the account of one eyewitness on board, and another in a steamer which passed the *Bertrand* eight days following the disaster, provide some information. The account of the former appeared initially in the *Davenport Gazette*, Davenport, Iowa, April 13, 1865:

> THE SINKING OF THE STEAMER BERTRAND—Our old friend W. Burrows, Esq. returned Tuesday evening from the Missouri River, where he was wrecked on the steamer Bertrand, on the first day of April, being bound for Montana by way of Fort Benton and having on board his daughter Mrs. Millard, and children, and

---

[5] Included were the *St. Johns, U.S. Grant*, and *Converse*. (*Daily Missouri Democrat*, March 17, 1865)

[6] A portion, if not all of the mercury, was consigned to a G. P. Dorris of Virginia City. The name "Dorris" appeared in faint red ink on the side of one of the nine containers of mercury removed from the holds in the summer of 1969.

several other lady passengers, some from the city. Mr. B says the Bertrand was snagged about twenty-five miles above Omaha and sunk in five minutes carrying down a cargo of groceries valued at $300,000, and becomes a total loss. Most of the effects of the passengers were saved, and the cargo was generally fully insured. No blame was attached to the pilot, as the snag was entirely out of sight. The disaster took place in the day time, amid pleasant, warm weather. About one third of the cargo had been taken out in a damaged condition when Mr. B. left. (Reprinted in: *Tri-Weekly Missouri Democrat*, April 16, 1865).

The second eyewitness of the sunken *Bertrand*, William Houston Gallaher of St. Charles, Mo., reported his observations in a journal—kept on his journey up the Missouri on the steamer *St. Johns*. His entry for April 9, 1865 follows:

Started early in the morning [having lain up for the night 22 miles above Omaha]. Commenced snowing about 8 Oclock. Geese and Pelicans and ducks very abundant. At 10 1/2 Oclock reached the wreck of 'Bertrand' Badly sunk to cabin floor, total loss except light freight from upper deck which was all taken ashore, and built into shanties for the protection of the crew. Passengers all up at 'DeSoto' eight miles above. While laying at the 'Bertrand' Fannie & Annie Campbell[7] came down to the wreck. Very much surprised to see us. They had all arrangements made for going on the 'Genl Grant.' 'St. Johns' left 'Bertrand' at half past eleven; ran onto a sand bar but sparred over in about an hour & a half. The balance of the day we made good headway. Laid up for night at wood yard. (Moss ed., 1963, p. 163).

In addition to W. Burrows, the mesdames Atchison, Millard and their children, and the Campbell sisters, the names of a number of other passengers, and possibly the name of two crew members in addition to Captain Yore, appear in the Herndon House Register.[8] The Herndon House, Omaha's largest and most prestigious hotel during the period, catered to both passengers and crews of steamers laying over. The initial entry for persons on the *Bertrand* was that of Captain Yore on the evening of Friday, March 31st, 1865, the day before the sinking. With Yore spending the evening in Omaha, it would appear that the boat lay tied up during the night and that the *Bertrand* had made almost 25 miles from dawn to 3 p.m. the following day, the time of its sinking.

While it is not possible to reconstruct conditions of the river at the time and place of the Bertrand disaster with precision, informa-

---

[7]Fannie and Annie Campbell were going to Montana to join their father, Major J. B. Campbell, who had settled near Gallatin.

[8]On permanent loan to the Greater Omaha Historical Society from Mrs. Alvin H. Goeser of Omaha.

tion in the diary of Abel Vanmeter gives some impression of the problems which Captain Yore must have faced on April 1. Vanmeter, enroute to Montana Territory in the steamer *Deer Lodge*, running
ahead of the *Bertrand* less than two days, noted in his diary of March
28 that the steamer had laid up 5 miles above the Boyer River in a
snag infested stretch of the river (Hamilton, 1972, p. 14). This would
have placed them in or very near DeSoto Bend. The following day the
Deer Lodge "proceeded up a short distance," and broke a flange on
the paddle wheel. The same day a rudder broke, also the result of
snags. On the 31st a snag caught the hog chain on the boiler deck and
carried the chain off. On April 1st they struck still another snag and
broke still another rudder (*ibid.*, pp. 14, 15).

Sometime in the afternoon of Sunday, April 2, several Bertrand passengers stranded at DeSoto Landing found transportation
to Omaha. In addition to Captain Yore, those persons checking into
the Herndon House, and specifically identifying themselves as having
come from the *Bertrand*, were Thomas Owens, H. E. Bixby and lady
and servant, Albert Rowe and J. C. Burns. Of the group, Owens and
Burns appear likely to have been crew members rather than passengers, inasmuch as both checked into the hotel again the following
weekend (Friday, April 7) along with Captain Yore, but this time listing St. Louis as their address. That they were engaged in salvage activity on the *Bertrand* during the intervening week seems plausible.

Early accounts of the total loss and nature of the cargo vary,
with some sources citing a figure of $100,000 *(Council Bluffs Non
Pareil*, April 3, 1865), and others as much as $300,000 (*Davenport
Gazette*, April 13, 1865). St. Louis interests were informed in one of
their daily newspapers as follows:

> A telegraphic dispatch from Omaha dated April 2d, announces the
> sinking of the fine steamer *Bertrand*, Captain James A. Yore, mas-
> ter, on the afternoon of Saturday, April 1st, at three o'clock.
>
> The dispatch states that the boat is a total loss. No lives lost. The
> boat was owned by Captain James A. Yore & Brother, and John G.
> Gopelin, and was valued at $50,000. Her freight was very valuable
> —consigned to parties in the mining district. The boat was partially
> insured. (*Daily Missouri Democrat*, April 4, 1865)

CONSIGNEES

Among the consignees of Bertrand cargo who were significant in the history of Montana Territory during the 1860's were Francis (Frank) L. Worden and Granville Stuart. The names of their companies and four others recorded during excavation of the holds appeared on readable shipping stencils on the outsides of wooden cases,

Figure 8. Frank L. Worden, pioneer merchant at Hell Gate (Missoula), Montana Territory. Worden was a major consignee of Bertrand cargo. (Photo courtesy of Northwest Reprographics Archives, Helena, Mont.)

kegs and barrels of merchandise. The firm names recorded included the following: Vivian and Simpson, Virginia City; Stuart and Co., Deer Lodge; J. Murphy, Ft. Benton; G. P. Dorris, Virginia City; Worden and Co., Hell Gate; and M. Kingman and Co., Virginia City. All of the firms appear to have been engaged either in general retail merchandising or wholesaling, or both.

Worden (fig. 8) was among the first settlers of the Bitter Root Valley and later became a member of the initial Legislative Assembly of Montana Territory. Planning to open trade at the Indian Agency at Walla Walla in 1860, he instead built a small log house at Hell Gate (fig. 9) which formed the nucleus of a small village, later moved 5 miles to the east and renamed Missoula (Stout, 1921, vol. 1, p. 223). Worden erected a sawmill at Missoula during the winter of 1864-65 and in the spring opened a grist mill and general store, no doubt intending to open his new business (fig. 10) with the anticipated stock of supplies from the *Bertrand*. Worden's activities in Montana Territory during the gold rush followed his employment during the '50s as clerk in the Indian Department for Territorial Governor Isaac I. Stevens. According to one of his biographers he then:

> was appointed and served as Postmaster at Walla Walla. Here he made the acquaintance of Captain Christopher P. Higgins, an enterprising citizen, and they entered into a co-partnership in 1860 to conduct a trading and mercantile business, and such other enterprises as their judgements should mutually approve, in eastern Washington, and came to what is now the County of Missoula. They established a trading post at Hell Gate Ronde, four or five miles below the town of Missoula. Upon the discovery of gold at Gold Creek, in 1862, they established a store at that place for the purpose of furnishing the miners, travelers and traders with goods. In 1863 they established another store at La Barge City, Cottonwood, or what is now Deer Lodge City, and kept an extensive establishment in that town. In 1864 they removed their mercantile establishment from Hell Gate Ronde to the mouth of the canyon, four miles up the river, where in addition to merchandising they con-

Figure 9. Frank L. Worden's first store at Hell Gate in 1860. The figure in the foreground is believed to be Judge Frank H. Woody, an early historian of Montana Territory. (Photo courtesy of the Historical Society of Montana, Helena.)

Figure 10. Worden's store at Missoula, earlier known as Hell Gate. Constructed in 1864-65, it was this business to which Worden's merchandise on the *Bertrand* was destined. (Photo courtesy of the Northwest Reprographics Archives, Helena, Mont.)

14

Figure 11. Granville Stuart, early legislator and merchant of Montana Territory, and a major consignee of Bertrand cargo. (Photo courtesy of the Northwest Reprographics Archives, Helena, Mont.)

structed a grist mill and a saw mill, the place being known for some time as Wordensville, but the name was changed by Mr. Worden to Missoula Mills, and subsequently to that of Missoula. This grist mill and one at Gallatin City, contemporaneously constructed, were the only custom mills for a long time operated in Montana, and they were of very great value to the farmers and early settlers of the Territory. (Sanders, 1896, p. 363)

Another of the better known consignees, Granville Stuart (fig. 11), operated a mercantile business and outfitted mining establishments at Deer Lodge during the 1860's. With interests in gold mines, general merchandising, and as an early legislator of the Territory, he would later become known for his contributions to the history of the Bitter Root Valley and environs. His early sketches became collectors' items and are among the first graphic representations of Fort Benton and the surrounding area (fig. 5). By March of 1865 he was advertising in local newspapers a dealership in dry goods, boots, cutlery, clothing, shoes, hats, groceries, and hardware—all items recovered with his name as consignee on Bertrand cargo (*Montana Post*, March 25, 1865).

The Stuarts, including Granville's brother and father, left Iowa for the California gold fields in 1852. When suffering from mountain fever in Utah in 1857, Granville made the acquaintance of Reese Anderson and a trader, Jake Meek, who took Granville and his brother James to the Beaverhead Valley in the winter of 1858. Here the men set up a trading partnership and, after sluicing gold on Benetsee Creek for two years, they began a mining and farming operation in the Deer Lodge Valley. Here the brothers became cattle barons, with interests in gold mining and general merchandising (Fletcher, 1961, pp. 22-26).

At least a portion, if not all, of the mercury originally intended for the gold mines was to have gone to one G. P. (General) Dorris of Virginia City. The name Dorris was written on the side of one container of mercury with a red substance that appeared to be ordinary

Figure 12. Virginia City in 1866 during the gold rush. (Photo courtesy of the Montana Historical Society, Helena.)

Figure 13. Murphy and Neel Co. at Fort Benton, consignee of a substantial amount of bitters on board the *Bertrand*. The store is shown immediately to the right of the bull train. (Photo courtesy of the Northwest Reprographics Archives, Helena, Mont.)

Figure 14. The wharf at Fort Benton in the 1860's, viewed shortly after the unloading of a riverboat. Front Street curves along the waterfront in the upper left hand corner of the photograph. (Photo courtesy of the Historical Society of Montana, Helena.)

paint. Unfortunately, upon exposure, the lettering disappeared in time, but was recorded in field notes when the mercury was recovered. In addition to other mining supplies, Dorris listed as having in stock clothing expressly made for the mining industry (Eds., *History of Montana*, 1885, p. 41).

John T. Murphy, another of the consignees, was engaged in the banking, mercantile and freighting businesses at Fort Benton, Virginia City (fig. 12), and Helena. A considerable quantity of the bitters and other alcoholic beverages on board the boat appeared to be destined for his partnership at Fort Benton, the Murphy and Neel Co. (fig. 13). By 1886, Murphy had merged with Frank L. Worden and the two opened a mercantile business at Missoula (Coleman, Ms., p. 8). Murphy was born in Missouri in 1842 and moved to Colorado as a young man. He arrived in Virginia City in 1864 with a wagonload of goods and set up a small trading and mercantile business. After moving his business to Helena in 1865, he expanded his interests to include freighting from Fort Benton to the mining camps. In later years Murphy expanded again and went into livestock, banking and real estate which made him a fortune (Armitage, 1961, p. 66).

While it should not be surprising, one of the more striking aspects of the transportation and merchandising business in the early history of Montana Territory during the gold rush, is the number of individuals and monopolistic firms that were engaged in both activities. In 1865, no less than four overland freighting businesses were transporting their own and others' goods from the teeming docks at Fort Benton (fig. 14) to the mining camps and villages of the Territory. All four had some interest in the *Bertrand* or its cargo. They include John J. Roe and Co., as part owner of the boat through shares in the Montana and Idaho Transportation Line; Stuart, King and Gillette, the former partner as a consignee; Thomas Ryan and John G. Copelin, the latter partner as part owner of the boat; and Worden and Co., a consignee of merchandise *(Montana Post*, April 1, 1865).

In the earlier accounts, the cargo is usually referred to as groceries, supplies for the mines, etc., but not until 1896 does a clear picture emerge of the much sought treasure trove. An Omaha newspaper article of July 22, 1896, relates the activities of four men who attempted to locate the wreckage of the *Bertrand,* ostensibly for the purpose of recovering 35,000 pounds of mercury and an unspecified amount of whiskey (*Omaha Weekly Bee*, July 22, 1896). The principal salvor of that attempt, F. M. McNeely[9] of Norfolk, Nebraska, was a young man of 17 who was present at the wreck site when an insurance firm sent a company of divers to recover the more valuable portion of the cargo. According to McNeely, a brother of one of the divers, a part of the cargo had been removed from the *Bertrand* when the salvors were ordered to the site of the wrecked *Cora II*, upstream several thousand yards from the *Bertrand (ibid.*). The *Cora II* was also headed for Fort Benton, struck a snag near Fort Calhoun on May 4, 1865, and was swamped in 6 feet of water (McDonald, 1927, p. 236; *Nebraska Advertizer*, May 11, 1865). According to the *Omaha Weekly Bee* account, by the time the insurer's salvors had finished their task with the *Cora II*, the *Bertrand* had disappeared, presumably below the silt.

Still another account mentions the presence of mercury aboard the *Bertrand*. Hiram Chittenden, in his annual report of the Missouri River Commission in 1897, listed the boat and cargo as a total loss, the latter part of which was reported to have consisted of "a large amount of quicksilver" (Chittenden, 1897, p. 3874). While a search of local newspapers following the 1896 attempt at salvaging the *Bertrand* failed to yield information on success or failure of the McNeely party, as late as 1936 stories were still being told locally of buried treasure aboard the boat. In an attempt to stabilize the channel in the DeSoto Bend area during that year, the U.S. Corps of Engineers hired a work force of from 300 to 400 men, some of whom ap-

---

[9]Others engaged in the search with McNeely were F. Hollingsworth and C. E. Daughty of Norfolk, Nebr., and B. F. Madison of Chadron, Nebr. The group engaged the services of A. J. Grover, civil engineer, of Omaha.

parently anticipated encountering the boat in the process of their earth moving. A Sunday supplement newspaper article briefly relates the activities of the Corps, and mentions the names of two men using "electric finders" in an attempt to locate the boat the previous year[10] (*Sunday Journal and Star*, April 12, 1936). According to that report, attempts at finding the boat were made nearly annually since the 1890s and that, in addition to the "earthenware carboys" of mercury, searchers anticipated finding 5,000 gallons of whiskey in oaken casks. It is worth noting that during excavation of the riverboat, no evidence of whiskey in oaken casks was found. Furthermore, the nine containers of mercury removed from the holds during excavation were of wrought iron, containing the present standard 76 pounds of mercury each.

[10]Norman Tilden, Washington County surveyor, and James Stewart, both of Blair.

Figure 15. Workmen removing cargo from stern holds of the *Bertrand* in the winter of 1968.

PART 3

DISCOVERY
AND
EXCAVATION

While the general location of the *Bertrand* was a matter of common knowledge in communities near DeSoto Bend, early newspaper and other published accounts contain very little information on its specific position of sinking. Assertions were made in these articles that the boat had been lost somewhere in DeSoto or Bertrand Bend, earlier known as Portage La Force. Other accounts contained such vague mention as a point 25 river miles north of Omaha City, or, near Council Bluffs, or, downstream from DeSoto Landing (*cf.* McDonald, 1927, p. 229; Moss ed., 1963, p. 163). At the turn of the century it was also common knowledge that the river had moved to the east of the village of DeSoto (Carr, 1903, p. 29), the remains of which can still be seen approximately 3 miles west of the Bertrand site near the nuclear facility of the Omaha Public Power District.

DeSoto, the old steamboat town on the Omaha-Decatur freighting road, was the Washington County seat from 1858 to 1866. It was depicted prominently on early maps, including the 1867 U.S. Corps of Engineers' sketch of the DeSoto Bend area made from the pilothouse of the steamer *Miner*[1]. The salvors, obtaining this map (fig. 16), approximated on it section lines, basing the configuration of these lines on the map scale, and the distance between and relative positions of the site of the village of DeSoto and the community of Fort Calhoun, the latter also depicted on the Corps' sketch. Assuming that the sketch map was reasonably accurate, and that the course of the river had not changed significantly between the time of the sinking of the *Bertrand* in 1865 and the mapping in 1866-67, the salvors were

---

[1] Entitled "Sketch of the Missouri River from the Mouth of the Platte River to Fort Benton, Made Under the Direction of Colonel John N. Macomb, Corps of Engineers, U.S.A." Original sketches on file: General Services Administration, National Archives and Records Service, Washington D.C.

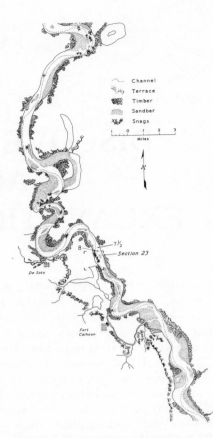

Figure 16. Colonel Macomb's 1867 sketch of the Missouri in the vicinity of De Soto, rendered from the steamer *Miner*. The corners of Section 23 were approximated on the map by the salvors. Note the heavy concentration of snags (x marks) noted by Col. Macomb, and the soundings of 8 and 7 1/2 feet of water in the channel directly north of the snags, the area in which the *Bertrand* was lost. (Photostat of Macomb's original sketch, courtesy of the U.S. National Archives, Washington D.C.)

thus alerted to those sections of the bend once cut by the channel of the river, information providing means of narrowing the area of their search.

SEARCH PARTY OF 1896

Following several weeks of archival research—directed principally at detecting clues as to the specific location of the boat—the salvors located the *Omaha Weekly Bee* article cited earlier in which the activities of the McNeely search and salvage party of 1896 were described. Appearing in the issue of July 22 of that year, the article reads as follows:

UNDER THE RIVER'S SANDS
WORK OF A HIDDEN TREASURE
WELL UNDERWAY

From the earliest recorded history, searching for buried treasure
has had a fascination for the seekers after wealth. Thousands of
men have spent their entire lives and millions of money have been
invested in enterprises of this kind. Fortunes of many millions have
gone down with ships and in many instances recovered after years
have passed away. No one form of search for lost treasure probably
has absorbed so much attention as this. For the amount of traffic
that has been carried upon it, no stretch of water on the globe has
swallowed up as much wealth as the Missouri river. Its shifting
sands and numerous snags have sent many a boat to the bottom,
and once located there, it is generally the work of but a short time
for the wrecks to disappear from view and the approximate location
of them is, in many instances, unknown. Of late years, since the
advent of the railroads, steamboat traffic on the stream has practically ceased, owing to its dangerous character. In the old days,
however, it was, with the exception of freighters' wagons, the only
means of transportation for freight destined for the far northwest.

From the mouth of the river to the head of navigation the bed of
the stream is strewn with these wrecks. In most instances the cargoes were removed at the time, in others portions were unearthed
after years, and in still others the boats and cargoes are still buried
beneath the quicksands of the treacherous river. The search for
these is revived every once in a while but in most instances the location is so little known as to render the chances of success very slim.

The largest boat that ever attempted the ascent of the river was
the *Bertrand,* which started in the spring of 1865 with a cargo of
mining supplies for points in Montana. The boat got along all right
until opposite the present village of DeSoto, in Washington county.
There it struck a snag with the inevitable result. This accident hap-
pened in April, 1865. The bend in the river where it occurred was
thereafter known as Bertrand bend.

Another Boat Around the Bend

On board the boat was a miscellaneous assortment of miner's supplies, the most valuable of which was 35,000 pounds of quicksilver.
In addition there was a considerable amount of that other necessity
in a mining camp—whisky. The insurance company which carried
the risk on the cargo was notified and sent a force of men to recover
it. They commenced the work and by the aid of divers removed a
small portion of it, when another boat, the *Cora*, on which the same
company carried the risk, was wrecked a few miles above where the
Bertrand lay. For some reason they abandoned the *Bertrand* and
went to work on the *Cora*. When they had completed their task
there, the *Bertrand* had disappeared in the sand, and the wreckers
gave it up as a bad job.

The affair was the talk of the neighborhood for some time and then gradually dropped out of mind. One man had not forgotten it and has ever since cherished the hope of recovering the valuable cargo. That man is F.M. McNeely, now a resident of Norfolk. At the time of the sinking of the boat he was 17 years of age and assisted his brother in the work of recovering the portion of the cargo that was saved, his brother being one of the divers, brought out by the insurance company. Lately he has secured the co-operation of F. Hollingsworth and C. E. Doughty of Norfolk and B. F. Madison of Chadron and they have employed A. J. Grover, a civil engineer of this city, to assist them in prosecuting the search for the boat.

Since the time of the accident the river has changed its course, as the Missouri river has a habit of doing, and the place which was then the channel is now two and a half miles from the river in one direction and a mile in the other, the river being to the north and east, the land being the property of J. E. Markel of this city. The first step was to secure the permission of Mr. Markel to prosecute the search, which was readily obtained. Next they sent to the department at Washington to secure accurate maps showing the course of the river at the time of the accident. In this they were more fortunate than they had expected. The chief of engineers of the army sent a map showing the meander of the river and the location of the wreck approximately, the records of the department being incomplete as to its exact location. He also sent a map made ten years later, which was guaranteed to be the exact location of the river at that time, but there was nothing to show that the stream had not changed in the intervening time and no mention was made in the field notes of the wreck or its location. The first map was made by Colonel J. N. Macomb of the engineers corps of the army.

Boring Holes in the Earth

From the incomplete field notes and the older map the location of the wreck can be established to within 300 feet in one direction and 1,000 feet in the other. The formation of the surface of the land at present, showing what has evidently been the bank of the river in times past, serves to bring its position down nearer to a certainty than the maps and field notes would indicate.

The four men who are prosecuting the enterprise are now on the ground, working under the direction of Mr. Grover. Various methods have been and will be resorted to in prosecuting the search. One of them has been the use of the dip needle. The quicksilver was put in lead casks, but there was a considerable amount of iron in the cargo and in the boat itself. The needle has shown some variations, but not enough to give Mr. Grover any assurance that the variation was caused by the proximity of the metal in the sunken boat, but he has not abandoned hope of locating it by this means, and a more delicate instrument than the one now in his possession will be procured and tried.

In addition to this the whole territory within the radius of variation from absolute accuracy in the old map and field notes is being bored full of holes to the depth of about thirty feet. These holes are being bored close enough together to be sure of striking the hull of the boat if the calculations as to its location are not very much at fault. From levels taken at present and from the old field notes Mr. Grover estimates that the hull of the boat is now in all probability about twenty feet below the present surface of the ground.

The promoters of the enterprise do not propose to give it up until they succeed or have exhausted every known means of locating the hidden treasure, which amounts to a snug fortune, if it can be secured. Mr. McNeely, from his own knowledge in working upon the wreck at the time the original efforts were made to recover the cargo, is positive that only a small portion of it was ever taken from the hull of the wrecked boat and is also positive as to the nature and quantity of it. Ever since that time he has cherished the hope of some day being in a position to prosecute the search in which he and his companions are now engaged and is very enthusiastic over the prospects of success. That he and his companions have given up their everyday employment and are devoting their time and spending money for its prosecution is evidence that they do not believe they are following up any chimerial story which has no foundation except in the imagination of some old-timer who gets it as a legend of the community in which he lives. The records in the departments at Washington also bear out their statements. That the *Bertrand* was wrecked near that point in April, 1865, is a certainty and it is also certain that the river has changed so that the location of the wreck is now far from the present channel of the river.

They hold that the original owners of the goods on the boat parted title when they accepted pay from the insurance company and that the insurance company has allowed its title to lapse by neglecting to make any effort to recover the property during all of these years, and if they can only uncover the hull of the old river steamer they have a small fortune in sight. They say they have faith enough in it to put a year's time and spend some money in securing the services of expert engineering assistance.

THE SEARCH OF 1967

That portion of the article which immediately attracted the attention of salvors Pursell and Corbino in 1968 involved the name of the owner of the land near that point on the river where the *Bertrand* was reported to have been lost. In reference to the sinking, the subsequent movement of the river, and the owner of the adjacent land, the article reads:

Since the time of the accident, the river has changed its course, as the Missouri has a habit of doing, and the place which was then the

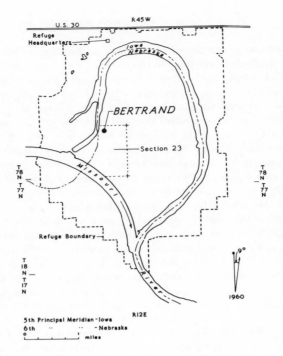

BERTRAND

Section 23

T 78 N
T 77 N

T 78 N
T 77 N

Refuge Boundary

T 18 N
T 17 N

9°

1960

R12E

5th Principal Meridian - Iowa
6th   "   "   - Nebraska
0 _____ miles

Figure 17. Present course of the Missouri in the DeSoto Bend area. Note new channel cut by U.S. Corps of Engineers to stabilize river (lower left). The *Bertrand* was found under the first terrace a few hundred feet to the east of the old channel.

channel is now two and a half miles from the river in one direction and a mile to the other, the river being to the north and east, the land being the property of J.E. Markel of this city [Omaha]." (*Omaha Weekly Bee*, July 22, 1896)

The salvors, assuming that McNeely, as the brother of one of the insuror's divers, was accurately informed as to the approximate position where the *Bertrand* went down, searched for legal description of Markel's property. This was found in the form of a warranty deed from Ford W. Grey and wife to Jacob E. Markel, and dated November 20, 1890. The deed described the boundaries of several parcels of land in Washington County, most of which were far enough away from the present course of the river that they could be eliminated as having minimal possibilities of bounding the Bertrand site. However, several parcels in Section 23 described by the deed, any one of which could have been cut by the river in the past 100 years, appeared to the salvors as having considerable potential in terms of the *Bertrand's* location:

> . . .the south east quarter of the south east quarter of section 23, and lot 3 in fractional north east quarter of the south east quarter

of section 23, and lot 2 in the fractional south half of the north east
quarter of section 23. . . .[2]

Referring to the Corps' sketch on which section lines had
earlier been approximated (fig. 16), it was evident to the salvors that
section 23 was not only cut by the river, but that the river in that particular area was shown in 1867 to have had a substantial accumulation
of snags, depicted by small x marks on the Corps' sketch map. Furthermore, the salvors noted that when the course of the river in the
1960s (fig. 17) was approximated on the early sketch map, the movement of the river appeared to have been to the north and east as described by the account of the McNeely search party of 1896. (*Omaha
Weekly Bee,* July 22, 1896)

A number of other clues given by the early newspaper account, and a foot traverse and aerial survey of the area, enabled the
salvors to further pinpoint the location of sinking. According to the
McNeely account, the *Bertrand* was described as having gone down
". . . opposite the present village of DeSoto, in Washington
County. . . ." Noting also that another boat, the *Cora*[3], was being
salvaged by the same company that carried the risk on the *Bertrand* a
few days after the latter had sunk, the salvors searched out the location of the old village and found it almost due west of the general area
of that portion of Section 23 that seemed most promising.

A traverse of the DeSoto Bend area, with attention to terrace
formation, along with inspection of the early Corps' map and air photos, made it abundantly clear to the salvors that the river had undergone a number of channel changes in the past 100 years. Prior to the
time the U.S. Corps of Engineers dredged a new channel to finally
stabilize the river in the area, at least three and possibly four distinct
shifts could be detected on early maps[4] and recent air photos. It was
with considerable relief that the salvors noted that the river did not
appear to have cut through that portion of Section 23 described in
the warranty deed transferring the property adjacent to the channel
where the *Bertrand* was reported to have swamped.

---

[2]On file: Register of Deeds, Washington County, Blair, Nebr.

[3]The account is in reference to the *Cora II,* listed by McDonald (1927, p. 236) as follows: "Stern-wheel, two engines, 15" by 5', two boilers, allowing working pressure of
144 lbs. Sunk by snag near Calhoun, Neb., about 30 miles above Omaha, in 1865, and
became a total loss except the boilers and machinery, which were salvaged." Yet another riverboat was known to have gone down in or near DeSoto Bend, *i.e.,* the *Stannard*
on May 13, 1865. (*Omaha Nebraskian,* May 18, 1865). See also listings for the *Bertrand*
and *Cora II* in Chittenden, 1897, pp. 3874, 3877.

[4]In addition to the early, unpublished Corps' map, others that trace the course of the
Missouri in the area include the following in the Nebraska State Historical Society archives: M 78-299, 1915; F 95, Maps, Location of DeSoto and Fort Calhoun.

THE DISCOVERY

With the search area thus narrowed to small portions of Section 23 in Washington County, the salvors next began a traverse of those areas with a flux gate magnetometer in hopes that ferrous materials associated with the boat would cause the instrument to react significantly and thus reveal its location. The use of flux gate magnetometers and gradiometers as remote sensing devices in archeological surveying is described by Aitken (1961) and Alldred (1964). In brief, the devices measure small differences in the magnetic field with readouts expressed in gammas, the standard unit measure of magnetic intensity[5]. In essence, the devices can be used to detect anomalies in magnetic intensity, *i.e.*, differences between the normal intensity of the earth's magnetic field in a given area and any object or objects which, within the area, affect such background intensity. Following several weeks of inconclusive results, the salvors finally hit upon the area directly over the buried riverboat, at which location significant differences of as much as 80 gammas were recorded between the areas surrounding the boat and the area immediately above the remains of what would subsequently be identified as those of the *Bertrand*.

At this juncture, the salvors established a 5-foot square grid system, taking a flux gate reading at intersecting points, and covering an area of approximately 190 by 60 feet. The resulting grid readouts were later tied into the datum established prior to excavation and removal of ship's decking (fig. 18). Upon excavation of the holds, it was found that the two areas of greatest magnetic anomaly corresponded roughly with those areas in the holds containing large iron plows and howitzer ammunition in the stern and large amounts of steel bar stock and kegs of nails near the bow.

With the flux gate indicating the presence of ferrous masses under the surface, the salvors proceeded to test the area with an auger, drilling a line of holes approximately 15 feet apart to depths ranging from 25 to 35 feet to intersect the two areas in which the flux gate recorded the heaviest concentration of ferrous materials (fig. 19). As the holds of the *Bertrand* were later excavated, it was noted that this row of tests had very nearly been placed along the centerline of the boat. Samples of cultural material recovered included boat wood, fragments of green glass, brandied cherries, brick, crating, leather boot fragments, lead bars and shot, a substance that appeared to be

---

[5]The device used by the salvors is the "Jaylander," manufactured by the Geophysical Instrument and Supply Company. Specifications include an oil dampened flux gate capable of detecting and attendant equipment which will record anomalies in a range from 10 to 250,000 gammas.

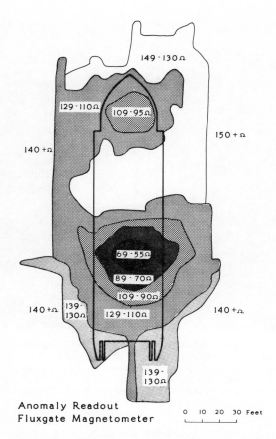

149-130Ω

129-110Ω   109-95Ω

150+Ω

140+Ω

69-55Ω

89-70Ω

109-90Ω

140+Ω   139-130Ω   129-110Ω   140+Ω

139-130Ω

Anomaly Readout
Fluxgate Magnetometer

0   10   20   30 Feet

Figure 18. The surface anomaly readout of the flux gate magnetometer depicted relative to the periphery of the *Bertrand*, below surface. The area strength patterns are based on the flux gate readings taken at 5-foot intervals. The areas indicating the heaviest concentration of ferrous material (lowest readouts) correspond roughly to those areas in the holds where most of the iron and steel was found.

tallow, tarpaper, and broken bitters bottles. With such evidence in hand, the salvors submitted a plan of excavation to the Chief, Midwest Archeological Center, National Park Service, before proceeding to uncover the boat.

The location of the *Bertrand*, in legal terms, is in the northwest quarter of the northeast quarter of Section 23, T18N, R12E, Washington County, Nebraska. Its position, in relation to the present course of the river, is within the loop of DeSoto Bend, approximately 300 feet east of the left leg of the bend and 3,500 feet northeast of the present channel of the Missouri which was cut by the U.S. Corps of Engineers during the 1960's in a major stabilization project (figs. 17, 20, 21). At the time of initial excavation, the boat lay below the water table and under from 20 to 28 feet of topsoil, silt, clay, cottonwood

Figure 19. The Bertrand site, before excavation. The salvors' use of this truck mounted auger, drilled to depths of from 25 to 35 feet, resulted in the recovery of boat wood and fragments of cargo. Note line of auger holes to right and rear of truck, an alignment which roughly intersected the magnetometer's readouts of heavy ferrous concentration depicted in figure 18. View to north.

logs and other wood debris. The boat was aligned at a bearing of 4 degrees (magnetic) and, on the basis of the 1867 Corps' sketch map, appears to have been headed directly upstream when it swamped and struck bottom. While the actual depth of the channel at the time of sinking is not known, the mapper on the steamer *Miner* in 1867 indicated a sounding of 7½ feet immediately upstream from the heavy concentration of snags in Section 23 (fig. 16). While we cannot be certain whether Captain Yore had taken evasive action to avoid the snags, it was noted during excavation that the rudders were in a hard port position, jammed against the 90-degree stops.

EXCAVATION PROCEDURES

During the time of peak activity, approximately 60 persons were involved in the excavation of the *Bertrand*. During the very early stages of the operation, however, the size of the crew was limited to from eight to ten persons, including a heavy equipment operator and his assistant, salvors Pursell and Corbino, at least one National Park Service archeologist, and a representative of the DeSoto National Wildlife Refuge.

Figure 20. Air view of Bertrand site, center foreground, view to south-west. Note recent channel cut by U.S. Corps of Engineers at upper left.

Figure 21. All cargo has been removed from the *Bertrand* in this aerial view to the west.

The initial attempt to excavate the *Bertrand* in March of 1968 was made with a dragline, used to remove the silt, clay and loam soils to a depth of approximately 15 feet directly over the boat. This operation resulted in immediate bank slumping or collapse when the water table was encountered 10 feet from the surface. The removal of the overburden, composed largely of sand and scattered layers of gravel and fine, silty clay (representing the backwater deposits of relatively recent floods) was accompanied by a movement of water to water table level, quickly filling excavated areas below the 10-foot level.

The salvors then used an 18-foot water pipe jet as a probe in an attempt to determine the actual depth of the boat, and to define its periphery. Contact was made with the decking at approximately 13 feet below the water table, and at this point the salvors used the dragline to remove silt from an area over the stern of the boat large enough to float a 6-inch dredging pump.

The dredging operation, conducted on a platform supported by pontoons, involved the pumping of water from the lake (left leg of DeSoto Bend) several hundred feet west of the excavation into the excavation itself to loosen the silt, whereupon the water suspended silt was pumped from the excavation (fig. 22). The dredge flow was discharged through a 1/2-inch screened hopper in an unsuccessful attempt to recover cultural material (fig. 23). Early in April of 1968 the excavation was enlarged to an area approximately 100 by 50 feet, approximately 20 feet in depth. The salvors then engaged the services of two divers equipped with SCUBA in hopes that they might get far enough below the water table to make physical contact with the boat. Limited visibility and the remaining layer of silt hampered this exploration phase of the operation, and continual bank slumping, the high water table, periodic rains, and clogging of the dredging tubes and discharge system during the summer forced the salvors to use a series of wells in an attempt to lower the water table to the level of the boat.

By August of 1968 the salvors had installed 30 well points around the stern and starboard side of the boat, the pumps exhausting the underground flow to the west into the lake. A 15-foot probing rod (3/8ths inch in diameter) was first used to determine the periphery and the standard hydraulic method was used to insert the wells. This involved the use of a 25-foot "stinger," an iron casing one foot in diameter, capped on one end and forced by its own weight and water pressure to depths ranging from 15 to 20 feet below the boat. The end of the stinger was then uncapped, the well point inserted, and the casing filled with gravel. The stinger was then removed, leaving the well point in a matrix of gravel. Flexible couplings were used to attach the tops of all wells to a system of header pipes leading to the pumps. Following insertion of the wells, the sides of the excavation

Figure 22. Initial sumping operation conducted on pontoons in the excavation immediately over sunken boat. Soils and silt in this first phase of the excavation were removed to the depth of the water table with the dragline and bulldozer at upper left.

Figure 23. The 1/2-inch screened hopper at right was used in an attempt to recover all artifacts during the initial sumping and dredging operation. The normal water table in the area can be seen in the excavation area at the center of the photograph.

Figure 24. The bilge hatch (opened by salvors) was among the first features of the *Bertrand* encountered. Evidence of earlier salvaging activity could be seen on the hatch in the form of holes drilled on the cover to enable the early salvors access to the bilge in the stern. Note portion of engine eccentric above hatch.

Figure 25. Side of soap case on which the words "Bertrand Stores" was brushed in stenciling ink.

were shaped by a bulldozer and dragline to minimize bank slumping. Ultimately, the well point system was designed to lower the water table to approximately 15 feet below surface in a large work area west of the boat where the crane, bulldozer, pump, and other heavy equipment could be used in close proximity to the boat. The series of wells immediately adjacent to the gunwales were set to lower the water table to a level equal to the lowest portion of the bottom hull. While this in fact was never quite accomplished, the table was ultimately lowered during the summer of 1969 to a point several inches above the lowest portion of the hull bottom where the cargo in the holds could be excavated.

By November of 1968 the water table was lowered to a point near the stern where the decking was encountered by the crane bucket used to remove overburden. Attempts were made to hose away the last few inches of silt and clay, although a good deal of hand shoveling was necessary to expose a small area of deck and the stern hatches (figs. 24, 27).

BERTRAND IDENTIFICATION

The first artifacts recovered from the holds through the hatches in the stern included several cases of Hostetter's bitters, boots, canned tomatoes, a plow, wine, black powder and primers, and a case which had once contained soap with cursive lettering in stenciling ink on one side which read "Bertrand Stores" (fig. 25). This appeared to be the first clear-cut evidence that the boat excavated was, indeed, the *Bertrand*. Further historical research and excavation would confirm the identification.

Perhaps one of the most telling bits of evidence that the salvors were actually excavating the *Bertrand* involved the recovery of a small chalk board (possibly meant for school) with the name "Fannie" engraved on the wooden frame. The object was found among other personal effects of a family (fig. 26). Fannie and Annie Campbell, daughters of Major J.B. Campbell, were on board the boat (Moss ed., 1963, p. 163). Furthermore, the name Atchison was noted by the author on one lot of personal possessions. A Mrs. Atchison, with children, were also known to have been passengers (*Montana Post*, April 22, 1865). In addition to this evidence, the remarkable similarity of the measurements of the boat to the registered dimensions of the *Bertrand*, the relationship of the sunken boat to the old village of DeSoto, and the position of the wreck site in relation to the land of previous owners recorded on the old transfer of property, combine to constitute substantial proof that the salvors had indeed found the *Bertrand*.

In addition to the items recovered in the early stages of exca-

Figure 26. The remains of what is thought to be Fannie Campbell's chalk board, found with the personal possessions of a family. The name was burned into the wooden frame with hot dies.

Figure 27. The water table had been lowered to the depth of the decking in this photograph of the stern, taken in the very early stages of excavation in the late fall of 1968. The large header pipes connected to the well points carried the ground water to the pumps which, in turn, evacuated the water into DeSoto Bend to the north. View to northwest.

vation mentioned above were a number of blacksmith's (engineer's) tools including a pitch cup, fire tongs, fragments of coal, brick, and the high pressure and cut-off cams of the port engine (figs. 24, 31). It is not known whether the latter were spare parts or had been removed from the shaft of the paddle wheel by the early salvors. However, even during the early stages of excavation during the fall of 1968 it was obvious that the *Bertrand* had been salvaged long before the 1968-69 attempt. It is known that an early eyewitness account of the swamped boat told of immediate salvaging activity. Portions of the superstructure were removed on the very day of sinking to provide temporary shelter for the crew (the passengers having been housed at the community of DeSoto). And within a few days the insurer had sent a boat with divers to salvage both the *Bertrand* and the *Cora II* (Moss, ed., 1963, p. 163; *Omaha Weekly Bee,* 1896). At any rate, during excavation it was abundantly evident that most of the driving mechanism, including the pistons, paddle wheel, and steam fittings (not to speak of the superstructure) had been salvaged long before the 1968-69 attempt.

With cold weather approaching during the fall and early winter of 1968, the salvors constructed a plastic covered A-frame as a

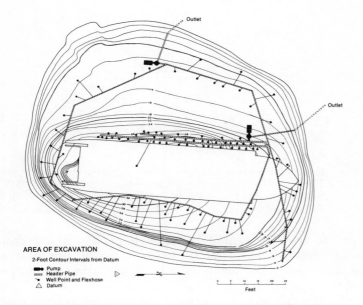

Figure 28. Periphery of *Bertrand* and limits of excavation in relation to datum. The isolines are drawn at 2-foot-deep intervals from datum. The figure also depicts the final positions of header pipes, well points, and pumps used to evacuate ground water.

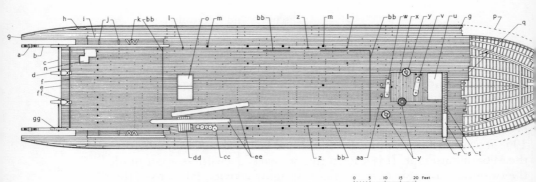

Figure 29. Surface of the *Bertrand* before removal of decking and the remains of the driving mechanism, superstructure, and hull: a. pillow block, b. inner cylinder timber, c. rudder articulating arm, d. master (balance) rudder, e. false transom, f. transom, g. guard, h. kevel, i. outer cylinder timber, j. cylinder cradles, k. cylinder timber braces, l. stanchion locations, m. hog chain brace locations, n. bilge hatch, o. stern hatches, p. guard periphery, q. forward port hatch edges, r. ash trap door, s. ash trough, t. fire brick on ash trough, u. ash pan, v. mud drum, w. steam drum, x. boiler flooring, y. paddle wheel flanges, z. hog chain grommets, aa. hand pump, bb. quarter-round moulding, cc. sharpening wheels (cargo), dd. scantling and hatch cover, ee. spare buckets (?), ff. stern posts, gg. wing rudders.

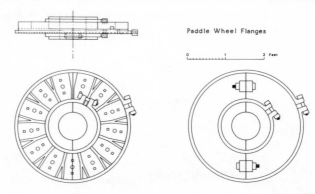

Paddle Wheel Flanges

Figure 30. Spare paddle wheel flanges found on deck near the boiler area. The parts show evidence that the *Bertrand* stern wheel consisted of 13 arms and buckets. End view at top, left; view to outside of flange, left; to inside of flange, right.

canopy to cover the stern of the boat in hopes of working through the winter months of 1968-69. However, the cold temperatures and equipment problems forced the men to discontinue their operations until the spring of 1969.

By late spring and early summer, excavation procedures were considerably modified. Approximately 150 well points were inserted at from three to five foot intervals around the boat (figs. 1, 27) lowering the water table to such an extent that the stern and bow portions were well above water. Ultimately, 210 such wells were inserted and an additional header pipe system and pump were installed (fig.

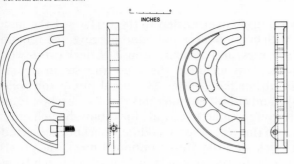

Eccentrics (Half Sections)
(Full Stroke, Left, and Exhaust Cams)

INCHES

Figure 31.   Full stroke (left) and exhaust cams found near the stern during excavation. The eccentrics were constructed in halves, just as depicted,
for easy adjustment and replacement.

28). At peak efficiency, the pumps were evacuating water at the rate of
4,100 gallons per minute, 24 hours a day, and had stabilized the table
at approximately 18 feet below its normal, 10-foot level. By June of
1969 almost the entire surface of the main deck had been cleared of
silt and clay and preparations were made to remove decking, mud
and steam drums, hog chains, stanchions and, following these, the
cargo (fig. 29).

FIELD CONTROLS

At approximately this time we established a datum on high
ground 62 feet to the east of the starboard gunwale from a point
slightly to the stern of amidships. The datum, a 4-foot pipe driven
perpendicularly into the ground, can be found approximately 5 feet
inside the west fence enclosing the public observation area. Its tip was
painted orange and selected elevations of ship's periphery, area of
excavation, positions of prominent deck features, etc., were recorded
from this point with the aid of a standard Gurley transit, and a rough
field map was made with alidade and plane table. From datum, the
positions and elevation of selected ship's features were recorded as
follows:

Bearing[6] *and distance:* to tip of bow (stempiece), 149.5 feet
at 33°; to midpoint of transom in stern, 84.5 feet at 341°.

Elevations: turn of bilge, stern, −33.24 feet; turn of bilge,
bow, −29.53 feet; nadir of center keelson (at a point 99 feet to the
rear of stempiece) −36.73 feet; zenith of center keelson (at a point 21
feet to the rear of stempiece) −27 feet; top of stempiece, −24.53 feet;
highest point of upper rudder assembly (starboard master rudder)
−21.14 feet.

---

[6]No attempt was made to declinate; all bearings are magnetic. Heavy rains in late
summer of 1969 resulted in considerable bank slumping near the original datum. For
fear the original might be lost, another was located in the field east of the boat. Its position from the original datum is 182 feet at 107°.

Upon removal of all overburden to the surface of the main deck, accomplished with crane bucket and hand digging, the remaining hardware, ship's fittings, and a small amount of deck cargo were mapped and removed. This included the mud and steam drums, spare paddle wheel hubs or flanges (fig. 30), hand pump for boiler filling[7], the full stroke and cut-off engine cams (fig. 31), firebox foundation, firebrick, ash trough, quarter rounds for cabins, hog chains, a single paddle wheel arm (fig. 32), a spare paddle wheel bucket, grinding stones, building brick, and the aforementioned mechanic's tools. Following these, the decking, remains of stanchions, and hatch framing were removed to allow access to the cargo.

While it may prove of questionable value to place all decking boards precisely in their original positions in the event a decision is made to reconstruct the wreck exactly as found, a recording system was devised to accomplish this. All decking was mapped[8] after individual boards were identified with plastic tape stapled to their upper surfaces. Identification letters and numbers for decking removed during the summer of 1969 were assigned as follows: The prefix letter "A" was given to all deck boards at the extreme port side with accompanying numbers in series beginning with 1 for the sternmost deck board. Thus, the first row of deck boards, end to end, farthest to the port (beginning with the sternmost board) were assigned numbers as follows: A-1, A-2, A-3, etc. The row of boards immediately adjacent to the A series, the second series of boards inward from the port gunwale, was assigned the prefix letter B, the third row of boards, the letter prefix C, etc. Following the prefix letter designation Z the letters AA, BB, CC, etc. were assigned. Hatch framing, the remains of stanchions and stringers supporting decking were also mapped as they were removed, and were assigned field numbers.

In general, removal of cargo in the holds was made following a standardized procedure (see Part IV). Ninety percent of the cargo was surrounded by a blue clay, decomposed Pierre shale, which was removed by shovel, trowel, and by high pressure water spray. Field lot numbers were assigned to the cargo prior to its removal to a storage area, and studies of the boat's buoyancy and wood drying rates were initiated (see Appendices C, D). Final photographs and scale drawings of ship's timbers were made following complete removal of cargo.

The weight or density study was undertaken primarily to obtain at least minimal information on the amount of time of exposure to the atmosphere the hull would require before it would float as

---

[7]Not to be confused with the "doctor," the main pump used when the boat was moving under steam. The hand pump recovered was used when the boilers were fired up but the boat was stationary. The "doctor" and most of the driving mechanism had been removed several days after the sinking by the early salvors.

[8]Field decking maps and charts, Midwest Archeological Center, National Park Service, Lincoln, Nebr.

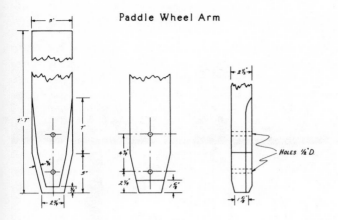

Paddle Wheel Arm

Figure 32. Paddle wheel arm found on deck near stern. With spare flanges (fig. 30) the part allows a reasonably accurate reconstruction of the paddle wheel.

a single unit, and to give engineers a rough indication of its weight should attempts be made to raise the boat in the future (Appendix C). Following a volume study, wood core samples of selected components were taken with a Swedish increment bore, and, with the aid of analytical balances and a computer it was determined that the mean density of the hull after approximately 4 months exposure to the air was 49.3 pounds per cubic foot, well below the density of water. Rates of drying the various components varied considerably, although it was found that when the water weight of most components fell to 39 percent of the total, they would achieve buoyancy.

The drying study clearly indicates that reduction of water weight to 20 percent of the total, thereby assuring minimal activity of fungi and bacteria, will require means other than simple exposure to the normal atmospheric conditions at DeSoto Bend (Appendix D).

By the time the cargo was removed, plans were made to protect the remains of the hulk in event that it might, in the future, be raised or exhibited in position. The holds were backfilled with silt to a level approximately one foot above the gunwales. A single layer of black polyethylene was then spread over the entire hulk, followed by six more inches of silt. A course of portable steel aircraft landing strip was placed over this layer of silt in the event that heavy equipment would be used to excavate in the future. The well point system, header pipes and pumps were then removed in stages, allowing the water table to rise slowly to its normal level. Several months after abandonment, the site appeared to be a small pond between two hills of backdirt at the bow and stern.

Figure 33. Storage of the Bertrand cargo. (Photo courtesy of the American Telephone & Telegraph Co., Long Lines Department.)

PART 4

THE CARGO

The enormous volume of the cargo recovered from the holds of the *Bertrand* during the summer of 1969, estimated at just over 10,000 cubic feet, necessitated the handling of all material in lots. Attempts were made at all times to retain the integrity of the contents of the containers and the containers themselves—removing them whole, with contents enclosed (fig. 34). Unfortunately, nearly 50 percent of the cargo (by bulk) was so badly crushed, particularly in the middle sections of the boat, that it was frequently necessary to separate the contents from the containers, and to assign both the same field number in the event a later cross check of material, and manufacturers' and consignees' stenciling seemed advisable.

The cargo, with the exception of that in the most extreme portion of the bow, was enclosed in a matrix of decomposed Pierre shale of varying consistency. This consistency depended largely on the amount of time the area of excavation had been exposed to the sun following the removal of decking, and the level of seeping ground water which, at certain points, escaped the suction of the surrounding well point system. In certain areas the clay was so resistant that it could only be peeled away from the cargo in thin sections with a square, sharpened spade or trowel. At other points it could be removed easily with the bare hands, or flushed away with water from a garden hose.

In the early stages of cargo recovery, systematic note-taking of the names of manufacturers and consignees was not made, it being anticipated that this information could be obtained at a later time. However, it was observed that the stenciling of certain lots of cargo exposed to the atmosphere for a few days began to deteriorate, becoming less and less legible. At this point, the decision was made to read and record all container labeling before the lots were wrapped in polyethylene. An estimated 40 percent of the stenciling on cases, kegs, and other containers was illegible despite attempts at removing the tightly adhering clay with soft brushes, brooms, cotton swabs and cloth. After a number of such unsuccessful experiments, it was found that a jet spray similar to those used in coin operated car washes removed the clay with the least damage to the names of consignees, manufacturers and wholesalers (fig. 35). Optimum results were obtained when the nozzle of the jet spray was held approximately 3 feet from the surface of the container, and the water directed at a 90-degree angle to those surfaces.

From the beginning of the period of cargo removal in the summer of 1969, it was apparent that a system of artifact recovery and field recording, quite unlike that established for most archeological sites, would have to be devised. In view of the rapid deterioration of certain artifacts when exposed to the air, and in anticipation of the need of preservators for a reasonably accurate account of the sequence and time of removal of the cargo to the open atmosphere, a field numbering system was devised to relay such temporal information (Table 1). Furthermore, it was hoped that a charting of the loca-

TABLE 1. Summary of field numbers assigned to cargo lots; general locations and dates of removal from the holds.

Assigned Field Numbers	General Location	Period of Removal (1969)
STDC 1-7	Deck cargo, starboard side	6/27 to 6/29
PSMC 1-219	Midship cargo, port side	6/30 to 7/4
PSSC 1-38	Stern cargo, port side	7/5 to 7/15
SSBC 1-140	Bow cargo, starboard side	7/16 to 7/22
PSBC 1-90	Bow cargo, port side	7/23 to 7/28
SSSC 1-224	Stern Cargo, starboard side	7/29 to 8/5
PSFC 1-177	Forward cargo, port side	8/8 to 8/17
SSFC 1-261	Forward cargo, starboard side	8/18 to 8/23
SSMC 1-363	Midship cargo, starboard side	8/24 to 8/30

tion of the lots would provide insight into the methods or practices of loading a riverboat. The system finally established involved the assignment of a series of letter prefixes followed by a number to each lot of cargo as it was removed. The letter prefix, e.g. SSSC, refers to the general location of the lot, *i.e.* stern cargo, starboard side. Its location was recorded on graph paper. The following number, 107, indicates that the lot was the 107th to be removed in that particular section of the hold. In those instances where many cases or boxes of an identical product were found together, and were removed together within a few hours, the same lot number was assigned to all.

The following inventory and gross description of cargo—with accompanying data on consignees, manufacturers and wholesalers—must be considered both tentative and approximate. Years of descriptive work remain before all the material will be of substantial comparative use to the historian or historical archeologist. Further-more, the varying speed of recovery by the salvors resulted in varying degrees of consistency and superficiality of identification. The pur-poses of this listing are limited, therefore, to 1) the presentation of a simple summary of the contents of the riverboat, roughly classified on the basis of use or function, the data derived solely from observations in the field, and 2) the listing of all shipping information stenciled or otherwise appearing on the containers. Thus, the main categories or classes of material are not unlike those that might be selected to make some order of a warehouse of supplies for a mid 19th-century mining and agricultural community on the frontier. These categories include 1) foodstuffs, liquor, and patent medicines; 2) textiles, wearing appar-el, and sewing supplies; 3) household goods; 4) mining supplies; 5) agricultural supplies; 6) hardware, tools, and building supplies; and, 7) miscellaneous. By so ordering the material it is hoped that some insight might be had into local economy and the demand of goods on the frontier at the time, and the nature of the businesses of the consig-nees.

By the time the cargo had been completely removed from the holds, the names and addresses of six consignees were recorded.

Figure 34.   Workmen removing keg of nails from bow hold.

A

B

C

Figure 35. Selected examples of burned and stenciled lettering on the exteriors of shipping cases; a. Vivian and Simpson, consignee; b. Kelly's

D

E

F

Bitters, manufacturer; c. Parker Brothers, manufacturer; d. M. Kingman, consignee; e. Stuart and Co., consignee; f. G. P. Dorris, consignee.

They appeared in stencils, or cursive and free hand lettering in brushed shippers' ink on the containers as follows:

—"Vivian & Simpson, Virginia City, M.T.," or, alternately, "V. & S, Virginia City, M.T."

—"Stuart & Co., Deer Lodge, M.T."

—"J. Murphy, Ft. Benton, M.T."

—"G. P. Dorris, Virginia City, M.T."

—"Worden & Co., Hell Gate, M.T." or, alternately, "Worden, Hell Gate, M.T."

—"M. Kingman & Co., Virginia City, M.T."

Although descriptions of classes of objects has scarcely begun, information on certain objects has been or is in the process of being published. This research is primarily the work of Ronald R. Switzer, former museum specialist with the Midwest Archeological Center. Where possible in the brief descriptions of materials below, a summary of his findings is included—specifically the bottles, howitzer ammunition, selected tableware (britannia), and the Maynard cartridges and primers. Within the next year or two several other reports on the textiles, buttons, ironstone "china," and tools will appear in selected archeological journals. Students of 19th-century glass bottles will find a thorough description and classification of bottles found in the *Bertrand* in Switzer's report, "The Bertrand Bottles: A Study of 19th-Century Glass and Ceramic Containers" (1974), National Park Service, Washington, D. C.

SYNOPSIS OF CONTENTS

The following list is a summary of all material observed and recorded in field notes as the cases, barrels and kegs were removed from the holds during the summer of 1969. Following this listing is another in which more detailed information on selected products and their manufacturers, shippers, and consignees is given.

Foodstuffs, Liquor, and Patent Medicines: ale, almonds, bitters, "Bourbon Whiskey Cock-tail," brandy, "Brandy Cock-tail," butter, candy, catsup, cherries (brandied), cherries (canned), chow chow, cod fish, cod liver oil, coffee, cream of tartar, currants, flour, "Gin Cock-tail," ginger, gooseberries, grain, grapes, hazelnuts, honey, horseradish, jelly and preserves, lard, lemon extract, lemon sugar, lemon syrup, lemonade (concentrate), "London Club Sauce," mackerel, meat (dried and salted and pickled, mutton, beef and pork), mustard (dried and bottled), oysters, peaches, peanuts, pecans, pepper, pepper sauce, pickles, pineapple, prunes, saleratus (baking powder), sardines, schnapps, soda crackers, spices, strawberries, sugar, syrup, tamarinds, tomatoes, wine and champagne, "Worcestershire Sauce," and yeast powder.

Textiles, Wearing Apparel, Sewing Supplies: bags (woven), bandannas, beads, belts, blankets, bolts of wool and silk, braid, buckles, burlap bags, buttons, capes, coats, dresses, dusters, gloves, hats, jackets, jute rolls, lace, leggings, muffs, needles, netting, pins, piping, plackets, ribbons, rugs, shawls, shirts, shoelaces, shoes, slickers, slippers, snaps, snoods, socks, suits, sweatbands, sweaters, table cloths, tassels, thimbles, thread, ties, trousers, umbrella covers, underwear, vests, yarn.

Household Goods: almanacs, book clasps, brooms, brushes, candles, candle molds, candlesticks, china (ironstone), churns (butter), clocks and parts, combs (ivory, hard rubber), cooking kits, cooking utensils, cups, cutlery, dye (indigo), glass goblets, griddles, hearth tools, ink, lamps and parts, matches, mirrors, pen holders and points, pencils, pie plates, pots and pans, soap, spice grinders, starch, stoves and parts, tallow, teakettles, teaspoons, waffle irons, washboards, washtubs and buckets, water tumblers, whiskey glasses.

Mining Supplies: blasting powder, detonating devices, mercury mortars and pestles, pickaxes, shovels.

Hardware, Tools, and Building Supplies: anvils, auger bits, axe handles and heads, barrel cocks, bellows (forge), block and tackle, bucksaws, carpenter's braces and squares, doorknobs, door locks and parts, dowels, draw knives, drill bits, files, froes (shingle splitters), hacksaws, hammers, hand saws, hatchets, keyhole facings, keyhole saws, keys, lead bar stock, lead seals, lead shot, levels, lock assemblies, mallets, mauls, nails, nuts and bolts, oil cans, padlocks, pipe and fittings, pipe wrenches, planes, powder flasks, rivets, rod (threaded), rulers, sash weights, saw blades, scales, screw hooks, screwdrivers, screws, sharpening stones, shot flasks, shot molds, sleighbells, spoke shaves, steel bar stock, tacks, tape measures, tar paper, thumb latches, tool handles, vises, white lead, window frames.

Miscellaneous Cargo: bullwhips, cartridges, cigars, coal, day books, gunpowder, howitzer ammunition, ledgers, paper primers, percussion caps, personal possessions, pipes (clay and briar), shoe repair supplies, tobacco.

Figure 36. Ceramic bottle which contained a domestic ale. Several varieties of these wheel-thrown, salt-glazed vessels were recovered in the holds.

Figure 37. Imported ale bottle from Amsterdam. The reddish-brown, wheel-turned containers are well known to collectors of 19th century ceramic bottles.

FOODSTUFFS, LIQUOR AND PATENT MEDICINES

Ale: Evidence of several varieties were found. Two broken ceramic bottles of one type appear to have been intrusive inasmuch as their necks were found outboard of the gunwales, and their bodies lay on the deck unassociated with any other cargo. That they could have been opened and discarded by the early salvors working on the vessel appeared quite possible. The other varieties were clearly a part of the cargo, and were shipped in cases of 12 bottles each (figs. 36, 37). Consignee: Vivian and Simpson, Virginia City. Bottlers' stenciling: 1) "COOPER & CONGER, ST. LOUIS ALE BREWERY," 2) "AMSTERDAM FOCKING WYNAND." Switzer (1974) describes the Cooper and Conger ale bottles as blown in two-piece molds with standard collar-and-ring, brandy type neck finishes. He distinguishes between six subtypes of wheel-thrown, salt-glazed bottles containing ale. The lower bodies of all the subtypes are cream colored; the shoulders and necks are pale to dark yellow ocher (*ibid.*). The Amsterdam specimens are wheel-turned, brown to reddish-brown, unglazed stoneware, well known to collectors and museums specializing in 19th-century bottles.

Bitters: A number of varieties were recovered, Hostetters predominant; 172 lots total (fig. 38). Packed in sawdust, 12 quarts to the case. Approximately 80 percent of the lots were recovered unbroken, contents intact. Consignees: Stuart and Co., Deer Lodge; Vivian and Simpson, Virginia City; G. P. Dorris, Virginia City. Manufacturers' stenciling: 1) "SCHROEDER'S STOMACH BITTERS, Louisville, Ky." 2) "DRAKE'S PLANTATION BITTERS" (fig. 39), 3) "DR. J. HOSTETTERS CELEBRATED STOMACH BITTERS, HOSTETTER & SMITH, Pittsburgh, Pa." 4) "J. H. SCHROEDER'S COCK-TAIL BITTERS, Louisville, Ky." 5) "KELLY'S OLD LOG CABIN BITTERS, Depots New York, St. Louis" (fig. 41). So extensive is the Bertrand collection of Hostetter's bitters that Switzer has counted 191, 12 bottle cases and distinguishes three varieties of bottles containing that firm's product (1974). Both the well known 22- and rarer 28- and 32-ounce bottles are represented. The smaller four-sided specimens best known to collectors were blown in two-piece molds and have slanting collar neck finishes and flat bases with dish-shaped depressions at the centers (*ibid.*). The Schroeder's bottles, known as "French squares" are olive green and were blown in two-piece molds. The Drake's Plantation bitters bottles are cabin shaped and amber-colored, the front and reverse sides of which have six relief logs above plain panels. The Kelly's Old Cabin bitters bottles are the well known, log cabin shaped specimens, and the Schroeder's Spice specimens are known by collectors and museum curators as "leg bottles."

Bourbon Whiskey Cock-tail: Bottled in 25-ounce bottles, 24 quarts to the case. Consignee: Stuart and Co., Deer Lodge. Manufacturers' stenciling: "BOURBON WHISKEY COCK-TAIL FROM A. RICHARDS." Switzer (1974) describes the amber and dark green bottles as having been blown in three-piece molds and exhibiting slanting collar-and-ring neck finishes.

Figure 38. Bottle containing Dr. J. Hostetter's Stomach Bitters. One hundred and ninety-one cases of this product were being shipped to the consignees in Montana Territory.

Brandy Cock-Tail: Packed 12 quarts to the case. Consignee: Stuart and Co., Deer Lodge. Bottler's stenciling: 1) "12 qts. BRANDY COCK-TAIL FROM C. A. RICHARDS, 91 WASHINGTON ST., BOSTON."

Butter: Packed in 50-pound kegs: contents badly decomposed. The kegs were banded with wooden strips, half round in cross-section, and were so softened that the staves had fallen apart. Specimen of contents taken for lab. Consignees: G. P. Dorris, Virginia City; Stuart and Co., Deer Lodge. Manufacturer's stenciling: 1) "BUTTER, DOREMUS, N.Y." (The names "C. PUPPY" and "C. REED" were burned into the tops of several kegs.) Four kegs bore the brushed lettering "Stores Bertrand" in stenciling ink.

Candy: Several varieties were recorded; all contents had leached away with the exception of a few fragments of nuts which survived in the bottoms of wooden cases; 27 lots total. Consignees: Stuart and Co., Deer Lodge; Vivian and Simpson, Virginia City; G. P. Dorris, Virginia City. Manufacturers' stenciling: "NEW MAPLE SUGAR CANDY—WESTERN CANDY FACTORY." Wholesalers' stenciling: 1) "S. H. BAILEY, WHOLESALE CONFECTIONERS, St. Louis, HOARHOUND" 2) "F. WALTER, WHOLESALE CONFECTIONER, CORNER MURTLE & 3RD ST., ST. LOUIS, EXTRASTICK CANDY, Net 24 lbs." 3) "FANCY CANDY FROM S. H. BAILEY, WHOLESALE CONFECTIONER, ST. LOUIS" 4) "50 lbs. LONGSTICK CANDY FROM S. H. BAILEY, WHOLESALE CONFECTIONERS, ST. LOUIS."

Figure 39. Drake's Plantation Bitters bottle. The distinct, cabin shaped containers retained fragments of paper labeling.

Figure 40. Artist's reconstruction of advertisement accompanying cases of Drake's Plantation Bitters. (Photo of original art, courtesy of the Smithsonian Institution.)

Catsup: Twelve bottles to the case. Manufacturers' stenciling: 1) "UNDERWOOD & CO., TOMATO KETCHUP, 67 BROAD STREET, St. Louis, Mo." 2) "Western Spice Mills TOMATO CATSUP St. Louis, Mo. One Dozen." Switzer (1974) identifies three types of bottles containing tomato catsup. The two Underwood specimens are faceted, containing 22 and 23 ounces (fig. 43), and the third variety, containing 9 1/2 ounces, is cylindrical and aqua colored.

Cherries, Brandied: A French product bottled in glass jars; packed 12 to the case. Consignee: J. Murphy, Ft. Benton. Manufacturer's stenciling: 1) "CERISES L'-EAU-DE-VIE, D.S.A.A.E." The cherries were bottled in transparent, aqua colored glass. Switzer (1974) describes the bottles as having been blown in two-piece molds; their sides expand out from the base to gently rounded shoulders. The necks terminate in slightly rolled collars.

Cherries, Canned: Packed in cans, two dozen per case. Metal cans badly decomposed. Consignee: J. Murphy, Ft. Benton.

Chow Chow: A table condiment, packed one dozen pint bottles to the case. Consignee: J. Murphy, Ft. Benton. Manufacturer's stenciling: 1) "1 doz. pints CHOICE AMERICAN CHOW CHOW FROM ALDRICH & YERKES, PHILADELPHIA."

Cod Fish: The vertebra and fins of cod, possibly dried and salted. The fish were packed in what appeared to be 50-pound boxes. Consignee: G. P. Dorris, Virginia City. Packer's" stenciling: 1) "BAY FUNDY COD FISH F. Snow."

Figure 41. Bottle containing Kelly's Old Cabin Bitters. The 25 ounce bottles are favorites among collectors.

Figure 42. Artist's reconstruction of Kelly's Old Cabin Bitters advertisement. (Photo of original art, courtesy of the Smithsonian Institution.)

Cod Liver Oil: Packed in five gallon tins. Consignee: G. P. Dorris, Virginia City. Wholesalers' stenciling: 1) "PETER E. BLOW, WHOLESALE DRUGGIST, 66 & 65 N. MAIN ST., ST. LOUIS, MO."

Coffee: Three types were recovered: one as a finely ground substance in small cans labeled essence of coffee, another as a coarse grind in boxes that appeared to have weighed approximately 25 pounds, and the third, a ground variety, in 32-ounce cans. Consignees: G. P. Dorris, Virginia City; Vivian and Simpson, Virginia City. Packers' stenciling: 1) "2 doz. cans 32 oz. JAVA COFFEE" 2) "-----MONDS ESSENCE OF CO-FEE."

Figure 43. Bottle containing catsup. The specimens were blown in two-piece, hinged molds and exhibit 18 flat facets around their bodies.

Cream of Tartar: Packed in 20-pound tins, eight tins to the case. Consignee: Worden and Co., Hell Gate. Manufacturer's stenciling: "PURE GROUND CREAM TARTAR."

Currants: Dried; packed in 25-pound boxes. Evidence of skins and stems remained.

Flour: Packed in 50 pound kegs; all contents had leached away. All kegs had collapsed and are badly fragmented. Consignee: M. Kingman and Co., Virginia City. Miller's stenciling: "CALUMET MILL, E. B. CARROLL & CO. CHOICE XXX FLOUR, CLARKSVILLE, MO."

Gin Cocktail: Packed 12-quart bottles to the case; 2 lots. Consignees: Stuart and Co., Deer Lodge; Worden and Co., Hell Gate. Manufacturer's stenciling: "FROM C. A. RICHARDS OF WASHINGTON ST., BOSTON, Gin Cock-tail."

Figure 44. French oval bottle, with prescription lip, containing essence of ginger.

Figure 45. Paper label affixed to can containing lemon sugar, an early version of instant lemonade.

Ginger: Six dozen small bottles of essence of ginger. Switzer (1974) describes these bottles as "French ovals," containing William Brown's "Highly Concentrated Essence of Ginger" (fig. 44). The necks of these transparent, aqua bottles end in a prescription type collar slightly flared at the base. Consignee: Worden and Co., Hell Gate.

Gooseberries: Packed in 2-pound cans, 2 dozen cans per case (badly deteriorated). Consignee: Stuart and Co., Deer Lodge. Manufacturer's stenciling: "GOOSEBERRIES, WM. H. THOMAS OYSTERS & FRUITS, BALTIMORE."

Grapes, Dried, White: Packed in 30-pound boxes. Only the stems, seeds and skins were observable. Sample taken for lab. Consignees: J. Murphy, Ft. Benton; Vivian and Simpson, Virginia City. Packers' stenciling: 1) "JOHN CLEMENTS LAYERS," 2) "ANTONIO DECAMPOS—ALAGA, S. ARIAS..," and 3) "Adolph Priest & Co., KHILINGA."

Honey: Packed in glass jars, two dozen to the case. Switzer (1974) identifies the containers as Gothic in style, similar to the many varieties of pickle bottles used by the Aldrich and Yerkes firm of Philadelphia. Consignee: Vivian and Simpson, Virginia City. Manufacturer's stenciling: "2 DOZ NET WHITE CLOVER HONEY from ALDRICH & YERKES, PHILADELPHIA."

Horseradish: Packed in glass jars, two dozen jars to the case. Switzer (1974) describes the bottles as having been blown in two-piece molds, with cylindrical bodies and short necks with sharp-edged, "blow over" finishes. Manufacturer's stenciling: "2603 Sixth Street, Cin. O."

Jelly and Preserves: Assorted varieties, usually packed two dozen jars or cans to the case. Consignee: Vivian and Simpson, Virginia City; Worden and Co., Hell Gate; J. Murphy, Ft. Benton; Stuart and Co., Deer Lodge. Packers' stenciling: 1) "NUMSEN, CARROLL & CO., 18 LIGHT ST., BALTIMORE," 2) "24 CANS PEACH MARMALADE FROM ALDRICH & YERKES, PHILADA.," and 3) "2 doz. qts. ASSORTED PRESERVES FROM M. UNDERWOOD & CO., BOSTON." Glass containers containing jellies or preserves are described by Switzer (1974) as 1/2 pint in volume; cylindrical jars with wide mouths, slightly flaring necks and thin rolled collars. Varieties of jellies include currant, apple, strawberry, raspberry, and quince.

Lard: Packed in tin containers, approximately 50 pounds each. Several were recovered intact, contents enclosed.

Lemon Extract: Packed 24 bottles to the case. Consignee: Worden & Co., Hell Gate. Manufacturer's stenciling: "BURNETT OF BOSTON."

Lemon Sugar: Packed 12 small cans to the case. All contents had leached away. A small vial of lemon extract was enclosed in each can of sugar. Labeling on cans describes method of making lemonade (fig. 45). Consignee: J. Murphy, Ft. Benton.

Lemon Syrup: Packed 12 bottles to the case. Consignee: Vivian and Simpson, Virginia City. Manufacturer's stenciling: "LEMON SYRUP MANUFACTURED BY MEYER & MUNSTER, ST. LOUIS, MO."

London Club Sauce: Packed two dozen bottles to the case. Wholesaler's stenciling: "2 Doz. PARKER BROS LONDON CLUB SAUCE, J. PARKER, N.Y. AGENT FOR THE U.S." The bottles are described by Switzer (1974) as containing 12 ounces of syrup, tall, cylindrical containers with long tapered necks and slanted collar neck finishes. The bottles, of pale, aqua-colored, bubbly glass, were blown in three-piece molds.

Mackerel: Packed in small barrels; apparently salted and dried. Vertebrae and fins survived. Consignee: Vivian and Simpson, Virginia City, Packer's stenciling: "G. O. PARKER DEP. INS. No. 1 BOSTON, MASS."

Meat: A good deal of badly decomposed meat was recovered. Some appeared to be dried beef and tallow in barrels; some was encountered with no evidence of containers.

Several kegs of butchered beef and pork bones were also taken from the holds. A specimen of meat, tallow, rind, etc. was removed to the lab and subsequently quick frozen for future study. Samples of this variety of meat were examined by the Armed Forces Institute of Pathology (Orthopedic and Soft Tissues Pathology Branch). Microscopic examination resulted in the tentative identification of mutton. Anti-ovine serum produced a precipitin reaction indicating that the specimen submitted came from an animal of the ovine species. An Agar gel diffusion test confirmed the serum identification. Stenciling on containers was not legible.

Mustard: Two varieties were recovered. One was packed in small, barrel-shaped jars, two dozen to the case; of French origin. The other was packed in pint jars with wide necks. Most of the contents of both had leached away. Consignees: J. Murphy, Ft. Benton; Worden and Co., Hell Gate; Stuart and Co., Deer Lodge. Manufacturer's stenciling: "PURREY & BAIRNES DE MOUTARDE, BORDEAU." The bottles containing the French product were blown in two-piece molds; the orifices were finished with small raised bands slanting inward to the mouth.

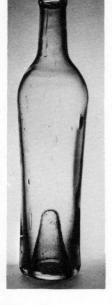

Figure 46. Bottle containing imported olive oil from France.

Nuts: Several varieties recovered including peanuts contained in burlap bags and boxes, pecans and almonds in barrels, chestnuts and hazelnuts in boxes. Consignees: G. P. Dorris, Virginia City; Vivian and Simpson, Virginia City; Worden and Co., Hell Gate. Stenciling of growers or packers: "ADOLFO PRIES & CO., NEW YORK PEANUTS."

Olive Oil: Packed in tall (*ca.* 9-inch) bottles of approximately 8 ounces; French origin; 24 bottles to the case (fig. 46). Consignee: Worden and Co., Hell Gate. Manufacturer's stenciling: POSSELFIL HUIL D'OLIVE, MARSEILLE, SURFINE." The highly distinctive olive oil bottles are free blown with deep conical kick-ups. The nearly cylindrical bodies taper to a smaller diameter from the shoulder to the base. The necks terminate in smooth, flat-lipped collars (Switzer, 1974).

Oysters: Several varieties were recovered. Packed in tin cans, 12, 24 and 48 cans to the case; tins are badly decomposed. Consignees: Stuart and Co., Deer Lodge; Vivian and Simpson, Virginia City; M. Kingman Co., Virginia City. Packers' stenciling: 1) "A. FIELD STEAMED OYSTER PACK, 209 W. Lombard, NEW YORK," 2) "2 doz. 2 lb. cans

CHESAPEAKE OYSTERS, NUMSEN CARROL & CO., 18 Light St., Baltimore," and 3) "2 doz. 2 lb. cans W. A. WENTZ & CO., FRESH COVE OYSTERS, BALTIMORE."

Peaches: Packed in 2-pound cans (badly corroded), 24 cans to the case; 18 lots. Consignees: Stuart and Co., Deer Lodge; J. Murphy, Ft. Benton; M. Kingman, Virginia City. Manufacturers' stenciling: 1) "2 DOZ 2 LB CANS Fresh Peaches from BRINKLEY & REEVES, BALTIMORE," 2) "Wm. UNDERWOOD & CO., ST. LOUIS," 3) "JOHN L. SILVER & BROS. Oysters & Fruits, BALTIMORE MD. Nos. 13 & 15 Water St."

Peaches, Brandied: Packed one dozen bottles to the case. Consignee: J. Murphy, Ft. Benton, Manufacturer's stenciling: "ONE DOZEN QUART JARS BRANDIED PEACHES, W. K. LEWIS BROS., BOSTON."

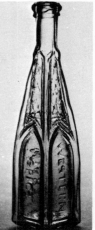

Figure 47. Gothic, letter paneled pepper sauce bottle.

Pepper: Packaged in small cans, 144 cans to the case. Fragments of paper labeling survived. Manufacturer's stenciling: "ALLEN MILLS, BLACK PEPPER, NEW YORK." Wholesaler's stenciling: "B. S. GRANT & CO., WHOLESALE GROCER, St. Louis."

Pepper Sauce: Packed in cathedral bottles, 24 bottles to the case (fig. 47). Identifiable contents include red peppers, numerous seeds, spices, etc. Consignees: Stuart and Co., Deer Lodge; Vivian and Simpson, Virginia City; J. Murphy, Ft. Benton. Manufacturers' stenciling: 1) "SUPERIOR PEPPER SAUCE FOR FAMILY USE, WARREN & CO., BALT. MD.," and 2) "SUPERIOR RED BIRD PEPPER SAUCE,----- NEW YORK"

Pickles: Packed in glass jars, 12 jars to the case. Several varieties were recovered; 25 lots (fig. 48). Consignees: Vivian and Simpson, Virginia City; J. Murphy, Ft. Benton. Manufacturers' stenciling: 1) "GHERKINS FROM GITHENS, REXSAMER & CO., DELAWARE MARKET, DELAWARE RIVER PICKLE & PRESERVE WORKS" and 2) "ASSORTED PICKLES" (from Githens, Rexsamer, etc.).

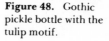

Figure 48. Gothic pickle bottle with the tulip motif.

Pie Fruits: Packed in cans, approximately No. 10 in size, two dozen to the case. Consignees: Stuart and Co., Deer Lodge; J. Murphy, Ft. Benton; Worden and Co., Hell gate. Manufacturer's stenciling: "2 DOZ CANS FRESH PIE FRUIT FROM RHODES & WILLIAMS, FRUITS & PICKLE WAREHOUSE, 107 So. WATER ST. PHILADELPHIA."

Pineapple: Packed two dozen cans per case. Containers bad-

Figure 49. Artist's partial reconstruction of paper label on one variety of French champagne.

ly corroded. Consignee: J. Murphy, Ft. Benton. Manufacturer's stenciling: "FROM ALDRICH & YERKES, PHILADELPHIA 2 doz. 2 lb. CANS FRESH PINEAPPLE."

Prunes: Found in a crushed barrel. Only the pits survived.

Saleratus: Baking soda, packed 12 bottles to the case; two lots total. Consignee: J. Murphy, Ft. Benton. Manufacturer's stenciling: "B. T. BABBITS PURE SALERATUS, Washington St., New York."

Sardines: Packed in small flat cans (approximately 100 tins to the case); badly decomposed. Consignees: G. P. Dorris, Virginia City; Stuart and Co., Deer Lodge. Packer's stenciling: "BOITES 100 1/4 PLUMETTE ET HOSTIN BREVETES, SARDINES A l'HUILE, ETEL Par. Auray MORBIHAN." Wholesaler's stenciling: "SCOTT & PERKINS, ST. LOUIS S. P. EXPS "

Schnapps: Bottled in pints, 12 pints to the case. Consignee: Stuart and Co., Deer Lodge. Bottler's stenciling: "WOLFE'S CELEBRATED SCHIEDAM SCHNAPPS, UDOLPHOWOLFE'S SCHIEDAM SCHNAPPS." Switzer (1974) describes the schnapps bottles as "French squares," containing about 14 ounces, green in color, with slanting collars.

Soda Crackers: Most contents had leached away; packed in what appear to be 25-pound boxes. Consignee: M. Kingman, Virginia City.

Strawberries: Packed in 2-pound cans, 24 cans to the case. Approximately 95 percent of the cans were so corroded that the contents had leached out; 9 lots. Consignees: M. Kingman and Co., Virginia City; J. Murphy, Ft. Benton. Manufacturers' stenciling: 1) "NUMSEN, CARROLL & CO., 18 Light St., BALTIMORE; and 2) "2 doz. cans FRESH STRAWBERRIES FROM FITHIAN & POGUE, BRIDGETON, N.J."

Sugar: Contained in 50-pound kegs. All contents had leached away, and most kegs had collapsed. Consignees: Worden and Co., Hell Gate; Stuart and Co., Deer Lodge. Manufacturer's stenciling: "CLARIFIED SUGAR FROM CHAS. S. KINTZING, ST. LOUIS, NO. 54 LEVEE."

Syrup: Packed in 10-gallon kegs; all contents had leached away and all containers were collapsed. Consignees: Vivian and Simpson, Virginia City; J. Murphy, Ft. Benton. Manufacturer's stenciling: "GOLDEN SYRUP 10 GALLS BELCHERS SUGAR REFINING COMPANY."

Tamarinds: Packed 12 pint bottles to the case. Consignee: Worden and Co., Hell Gate. Manufacturer's stenciling: "ONE DOZ. PINTS TAMARINDS FROM W. K. LEWIS & BROS., BOSTON."

Tomatoes: Packed in 2-pound cans, 2 dozen cans per case. The cans were badly corroded, although a few may be restorable. Consignees: Stuart and Co., Deer Lodge; M. Kingman and Co., Virginia City. Manufacturer's stenciling: "2 DOZ CANS FRESH TOMATOES FROM BRINKLEY & REEVES, BALTIMORE."

Wine and Champagne: Packed in wicker baskets, wooden cases and barrels. Approximately 70 percent of the bottles was recovered unbroken although most paper labeling had disintegrated (fig. 49). Very little data on bottlers survived. Several varieties of white and red wine were bottled in pints and quarts; one variety of red was bottled in 2-gallon bottles encased in a wicker carrier. Consignees: Vivian and Simpson, Virginia City; J. Murphy, Ft. Benton. Bottlers' stenciling: 1) "GREEN SEAL," 2) "HEIDSIECK AND RIEMS CO.," 3) "PRINCE IMPERIAL---E. V. H.," 4) "VEP & CO, 76," 5) "AMERICAN WINE, SPARKLING CATAWBA, St. Louis, Mo.," and 6) "1 doz. qts. CHAMPAGNE, J. W. B., N. Y. CIDER, DEPOT 92 & 94 CEDAR ST." Several types of subtypes of wine and champagne bottles have been classified by Switzer (1974). The thick green bottles are of the blown-in-mold type and were rotated in the molds while the glass was still molten. In addition to demijohns, several odd-sized specimens such as "splits" were recovered. These smaller, 12

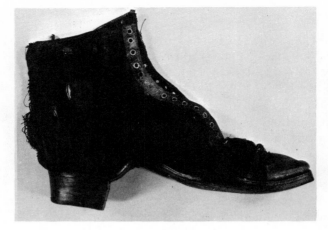

Figure 50. Woman's dress shoe with fabric top.

1/2-ounce bottles were also blown-in-mold with high kick-ups in their bases.

Worcestershire Sauce: Packed 1 dozen bottles to the case. Consignee: Stuart and Co., Deer Lodge. Manufacturer's stenciling: "1 doz. bottles WORCESTERSHIRE SAUCE FROM E. F. DIXIE, N. Y." The bottles are a transparent, aqua-colored type with cylindrical bodies. They were made in two-piece molds and were finished with a triple ring collar bearing a flat lip. Raised lettering on the tops of the glass stoppers reads: "LEA & PERRINS (Switzer, 1974).

Yeast Powder: Packed in large barrels, approximately 200 small cans to the lot. Fragments of paper labeling survived. Consignees: G. P. Dorris, Virginia City; Stuart and Co., Deer Lodge. Manufacturer's stenciling: "INFALLIBLE YEAST POWDER."

TEXTILES AND WEARING APPAREL

Boots and Shoes: Approximately 700 pairs of boots and shoes were recovered from the holds; most were packed 12 or 24 pairs to the case. Included are hobnailed mining boots, cavalry boots, dress shoes and boots for men and women, children's and baby shoes (figs. 50-54). Most were made on lasts which allowed the shoes to be worn on either foot. Most were sewn with linen thread which had disintegrated. Consignees: Worden and Co., Hell Gate; Vivian and Simpson, Virginia City; G.P. Dorris, Virginia City. Manufacturers' stenciling: 1) "24 prs. IDAHO MINING BOOTS 1/2 D. Sole Oil Treed Fancy Nails," 2) "60 prs. DONELSON BOOTS FROM M. C. DIZER & CO., WEYMOUTH, MASS.," 3) "1

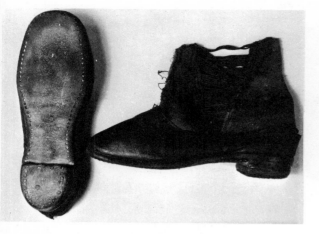

Figure 51. Children's shoes with expanding tops.

Figure 52. Children's shoes with brass scuff plates.

Figure 53. Men's dress shoes with expanding tops (Congress gaiters).

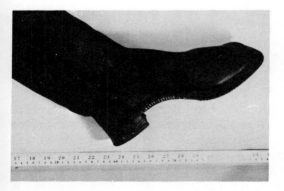

Figure 54. Miner's boot with knee protector top.

Figure 55. Example of men's felt dress hat found in cargo (planter style).

Figure 56. Close-up view of woolen fabric from miner's shirt.

Figure 57. Men's woolen trousers.

DOZ. PRS MENS SLAUGHTER BOOTS FROM W. S. BATCHELDER, HOLLISTON, MASS.," 4) "MENS IDAHO MINING BOOTS FROM LAFLIN, COBURN MASS.," 5) "12 PRS. GENTS FINE CALF BOOTS 1/2 WELTED FROM ALDEN & HOWARD, RANDOLPH, MASS.," 6) "12 PRS. OUR BEST BOYS KIP BOOTS, PATNA, FROM GEO. C. WALLS, BOSTON," and 7) "BOOTS FROM S. WALKER & CO., BOSTON." Wholesalers' stenciling: 1) "J. R. LIONBERGER & CO. NO. 71 MAIN STREET, ST. LOUIS," 2) "12 PAIRS MEN'S HOBNAIL BOOTS FROM WILLIAM E. NORTH, 79 MAIN ST., ST. LOUIS," 3) "24 PAIRS LADIES' BOOTS FROM WILLIAM E. NORTH, 79 MAIN ST., ST. LOUIS," 4) "FROM J. F. SCHIEFER SADDLERY AND LEATHER WHOLESALE HOUSE, 90 MAIN ST., ST. LOUIS," and 5) "12 PRS. FINE CALF DRESS BOOTS WELT FROM WILLIAM E. NORTH, 79 Main ST., ST. LOUIS."

Hats, Felt: Several varieties and sizes recovered. Most were black or dark grey, with wide brims and leather sweat bands (fig. 55). Consignee: G. P. Dorris, Virginia City. Manufacturer's stenciling: "From KIMBROUGH'S HATS, CAPS, ---NNETS & CO., ST. LOUIS."

Textiles: Approximately 1,200 cubic feet of textiles were recovered. Much of it was removed in apparently excellent condition, but a good deal was so decomposed that it fell apart at the slightest touch. All lots were wrapped in polyethylene and were placed under refrigeration at 40° F. Animal products, including wool and silk, appeared to survive the best (figs. 56-63). What appeared to be cotton and burlap around peanuts and shovels was badly decomposed. Little attempt was made in the field to identify the textiles. Consignees: Vivian and Simpson, Virginia City; G. P. Dorris, Virginia City. Wholesalers' and manufacturers' stenciling: 1) "Mfg. by YOUNG & CO., ST. LOUIS," 2) "BAST & POLLOCK DRY GOODS, No. 150 Main St., St. Louis," 3) "WILLIAM YOUNG & CO., No. 106 Main St., St. Louis," 4) "WILLIAM NORTH & CO., 100 MAIN ST., ST. LOUIS," and 5) "CAMPBELL'S DRY GOODS—INDIAN GOODS, St. Louis, Mo." The list of textiles and wearing apparel presented in the synopsis of contents was abstracted from a report prepared at the Midwest Archeological Center, National Park Service, following two years of work on the material. Approximately 3,000 complete items of clothing and over 5,000 fragments were processed in the laboratory.

Figure 58.
Men's woolen shirt.

Figure 59.   Woolen ankle-length stockings.

Figure 60.   Men's lined raincoat.

HOUSEHOLD GOODS

Brooms: None recoverable intact; near complete disintigration. Specimens of handles and straw taken for lab. Apparently shipped 12 to a burlap wrapped bundle.

Candle Molds and Accessories: Several lots containing equipment for candlemaking were recovered. Although the mold tubes, stoves, and pots and pans were badly corroded, several should be restorable. Consignee: G. P. Dorris, Virginia City. Manufacturer's stenciling: "BERNS H--DEAHN."

Candles: Packed one gross to the case. Approximately 20 percent was removed in excellent condition, although wicks had disintegrated. Most specimens were badly decomposed. Consignees: Vivian and Simpson, Virginia City; J. Murphy, Ft. Benton; M. Kingman and Co., Virginia City. Manufacturers' stenciling: 1) "GOODWIN AND ANDERSON STAR

Figure 61. Woman's knit shawl with tassels.

Figure 62. Woman's knit snood with tassel.

CANDLES, St. Louis, Mo.," 2) "N. SCHAEFFER & CO. STAR CANDLES, St. Louis, Mo.," and 3) "SOLAR SPERM CANDLES, SCHAEFFER & CO., ST. LOUIS, MO."

Clocks and Clock Parts: One clock was found in the personal possessions of the Atchison family; another shipment appeared to be clock parts and, another, six clocks in one case. Manufacturer's stenciling: "UNION GLIDE-----"

Combs: Several varieties recovered. Materials include ivory, wood, and hard rubber. Many were packed with textiles.

Cooking Kits: Four sets of cooking kits, each of which includes a kettle, coffee pot, tea pot, soup pot and lids. Consignee: G. P. Dorris, Virginia City.

Cooking Utensils: Packed with other goods, including hardware and ironstone. The utensils include coffee grinders and parts, wine press, copper bucket, iron cauldron, pans, flatirons and skillets, teakettles, coffee pots and baking pans.

Figure 63.
Bolt of black silk.

China: Ironstone. Packed in barrels along with other dinnerware, silverware, lamps, water glasses, casters, etc. The contents include plates, cups, pitchers, candlesticks, compotes, and bowls (fig. 64).

Churns, Butter: Wooden, with attached mercury thermometer (fig. 65). Revolving, hand-crank variety.

Cutlery: Packed with hardware. They include spoons, knives, forks and scissors.

Dye: One variety of indigo was on board. The containers were stained a deep blue, and the material had leached away. Consignee: Vivian and Simpson, Virginia City. Manufacturer's stenciling: "DOMESTIC INDIGO 10 lbs. STRODE RUBEN & CO., St. Louis, SPAUL E."

Glass Goblets: Packed 48 to the case. Badly damaged; less than 20 percent survived intact.

Ink: Two types recovered, a green ledger ink imported from London, and a blue-black variety for use in school desks. Consignee: Vivian and Simpson, Virginia City. Manufacturers' stenciling: 1) "24 PINTS GREEN ARNOLD'S INK, R & J Arnold, London," and 2) "4 DOZ. BOTTLES INK, R. B. SNOW, ST. LOUIS, MO." The domestic ink was contained in small, 1 1/2-ounce, octagonal, transparent glass bottles. The London variety was contained in cylindrical, wheel-thrown stoneware bottles containing about 14 ounces. These were brown salt glazed with flat, unglazed bases (Switzer, 1974).

Figure 64. Ironstone china, rosebud design.

Figure 65. Butter churn, revolving paddle variety.

Figure 66.
Lamp reconstructed from parts found in cargo.

Lamp Bases: Badly shattered; approximately 10 percent recovered intact (fig. 66). Several types and colors of glass represented. Most were found in large barrels with wick assemblies and flues.

Lamp Flues: Approximately 25 percent recovered unbroken. The glass flues ranged in height from 3 to 12 inches, and were shipped either in cases of 144, 72, or with other materials, including lamp bases, wick assemblies, and ironstone china. Consignees: Vivian and Simpson, Virginia City; Stuart and Co., Deer Lodge; G. P. Dorris, Virginia City. Manufacturers' stenciling: 1) "12 doz. No. 1 XX CHIMNEYS, ANNEALED FROM E. DONALSON CO.," and 2) "6 doz. No. 2 EXC. CHIMNEYS, ANNEALED FROM E. DONALSON CO."

Lamp Reflectors and Wall Brackets: Hardware generally packed with lamp flues, bases, and wick assemblies.

Lamp Wick Assemblies: Packed with lamp flues and bases.

Matches: Boxes of approximately 500, packed 48 boxes to the case (fig. 67). Most lots were badly crushed and it was usually necessary to separate contents from cases; 16 lots. Consignees: Stuart and Co., Deer Lodge; Vivian and Simpson, Virginia City; Worden and Co., Hell Gate; G. P. Dorris, Virginia City. Manufacturer's stenciling: "TELEGRAPH MATCHES, A. EICHELE, ST. LOUIS."

Mirrors: Found both in personal effects, and in shipments of six to the case. The mirrors, set in wooden frames, were fragmented.

Figure 67.   Artist's reconstruction of label on matchboxes.

Sewing Supplies: Found with personal possessions of the Atchison family. The supplies include thread, buttons, braid, pins, needles, and ribbon.

Shoe polish: Packed in circular tins; approximately 300 tins to the case. Consignee: Stuart and Co., Deer Lodge.

Soap: Evidence of several varieties recovered; all contents had leached away; 16 lots total. Consignees: Vivian and Simpson, Virginia City; Worden and Co., Hell Gate. Manufacturers' stenciling: 1) "----NCH & CO., St. Louis, Mo., 60 BARS, 60 LBS GERMAN SOAP," 2) "60 BARS PALM SOAP, N. Schaeffer & CO., St. Louis," 3) "80 BARS 60 LBS N. Schaeffer & CO., OLEINE OXIDE SOAP, St. Louis," and 4) "18 lbs. CASTILE SOAP, N. SCHAEFFER & CO., St. Louis."

Starch: Apparently packed in 45 pound boxes. All contents had leached away. Manufacturers' stenciling: 1) "----N ERKENBRECHER REFINED PEARL STARCH, Cin. O.," and 2) "WATT STARCH WORKS, Unchemical Pure Pearl Starch."

Stoves and Stove Parts: Packed with other goods, including hardware and dinnerware. The parts include iron fittings and stovepipe.

Tallow: One lot shipped in 12-inch "wheels," three inches thick; 10 wheels to the case, and another lot in a small (33-gallon) barrel.

Washboards: Most were recovered in fragmented condition; metal rubbing surface deteriorated. Most lots appeared to have been tied or wrapped in bundles of six. Consignees: J. Murphy, Ft. Benton; Vivian and Simpson, Virginia City. Manufacturers' stenciling: 1) "JOSEPH W. WAYNE Sole Proprietor, Manufacturer of O. RICE'S IMPROVED WASHBOARD, PATENTED OCT. 10, Cin. O.," and 2) "WASHBURN & CO., CHICAGO, ILL."

Washtubs and Buckets: Several sizes recovered, usually telescoped three or twelve to a lot. The exteriors of the oaken buckets were painted green, blue and red. The majority was banded with wrought iron. Many were recovered with wire bails.

Water Tumblers: Packed 24 glasses to the case; approximately 50 percent was recovered intact.

Whiskey Glasses: Packed 144 to the case; 80 percent broken; ca. 6 ounce. Consignee: Worden and Co., Hell Gate. Wholesaler's stenciling: "-. Garnea - & Co., ST. LOUIS."

Figure 68. One of the nine containers of mercury found in the forward holds of the *Bertrand*. The wrought iron vessels contained the standard 76 pounds of mercury each.

Writing Supplies: Included with other objects such as billfolds, etc. Pencils, pen points, pen holders, book clasps, ledgers, day books, and leather book covers.

MINING SUPPLIES

Black Powder: Recovered in small kegs with wire and wooden bails. These lots weighed approximately 10 pounds when dry. Much of the powder had leached away. Grades F to FFF. Consignee: G. P. Dorris, Virginia City. Manufacturer's stenciling: "LAFLIN SMITH & BOIL, SAUGERTIES, NEW YORK."

Mercury: Contained in nine wrought iron cylindrical containers with screw carrier cap (fig. 68). The containers, with enclosed contents, ranged in weight from 85 to 90 pounds. Stamped die of container weight visible. Eight of the containers were recovered in a 5- by 10-foot square area approximately 15 feet to the rear of the stempiece. Five containers were recovered from 2 to 8 inches above the hold planking, surrounded by sand. Three were found directly on the hold planking underneath approximately 600 pounds of steel bar stock. One container was found in the back dirt, apparently excavated from the hold by the crane bucket when removing sand. Consignee: One container bore the name "G. P. Dorris" written in red paint along the cylinder side.

Mortars and Pestles: Four sets in one case. Cast iron; weight about 30 pounds each. These appear to be assayers' pestles and mortars. Consignee: G. P. Dorris, Virginia City.

Pickaxes: Packed in lots of 24 or 48 to the case (fig. 69).

Pick Handles: Packed 48 to the case or burlap bundle.

Shovels: Both D-handle and straight handle varieties recovered. Approximately 80 percent of all shovels were recovered intact. The specimens appeared to have been wrapped in burlap, 12 shovels to the bundle.

AGRICULTURE SUPPLIES

Axle Grease: Packed in cylindrical tins, approximately 5 pounds each. Consignee: Stuart and Co., Deer Lodge. Wholesaler's stenciling: "FROM L. Z----."

Forks, Garden and Hay: Several varieties and sizes recovered, including long handled hay forks and four-tined garden (potato) forks, shipped 12 to a bundle.

Figure 69.   Pickax heads.

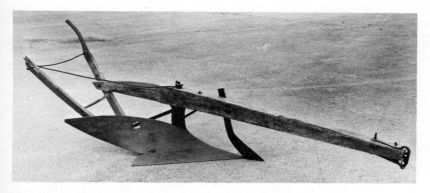

Figure 70.   Plow manufactured by Blunden Koenig & Co. of St. Louis.

Harness: Appears to be leather harness for a horse; in fragmented condition.

Hoes, Garden: Shipped 12 to a bundle; the wood handles were badly decomposed.

Plow and Cultivator Frames: Several varieties and sizes recovered; many were badly crushed, although restoration of the majority should be possible. Manufacturers' stenciling: 1) "J GARNETT & CO., ST. LOUIS, MO.," and 2) "TOBEY & ANDER, PEORIA, ILL."

Plows and Plow Blade Assemblies: Several large (*ca.* 18-inch blade) plows with tongues attached, and a number of smaller plow blade assemblies (fig. 70). A number were recovered with attached disc sodcutters. Manufacturer's stenciling on the tongues: "BLUNDEN   KOENIG & CO., ST. LOUIS, MO."

Scythes: Two-handed, 4-foot blade variety.

BUILDING SUPPLIES

Axe Handles: Packed 12, 24 and 48 to the bundle (burlap wrapped) or wooden case. Consignees: Vivian and Simpson, Virginia City; Worden and Co., Hell Gate.

Axe Heads: Shipped 12 and 24 to the case. Consignees: Stuart and Co., Deer Lodge; Worden and Co., Hell Gate. Manufacturer's stenciling: "L. BLOOD'S STEEL AXES, YANKEE PATTERN." Wholesaler's stenciling: "NEWLAND MANLEY HARDWARE, PHILA."

Hardware and Tools: Miscellaneous hardware packed approximately 150 pounds to the box. Most lots contained a variety of small tools and building materials. Several lots may have been shipments from mail order houses. Consignees: Stuart and Co., Deer Lodge; G. P. Dorris, Virginia City;

Worden and Co., Hell Gate. Wholesalers' stenciling: 1) "FROM NEWLAND MANLEY HARDWARE, PHILA..," 2) "A. F. SHAPLEIGH & CO., DEALERS IN HARDWARE AND CUTLERY, ST. LOUIS," and 3) "PRATT & FOX, IMPORTERS, DEALERS IN HARDWARE AND CUT-LERY, ST. LOUIS." The listing of hardware in the synopsis of contents was made from field notes and is limited to that which was observable while the cargo was being removed.

Lead Bar Stock: One-eighth pound bars, packed 144 bars to the case. Consignee: Worden and Co., Hell Gate. Manufac-turer's stenciling: "ST. LOUIS SHOT TOWER CO., ST. LOUIS, MO."

Lead, White: Packed in 25 pound kegs. Contents generally remained intact. Consignee: Worden and Co., Hell Gate. Manufacturer's stenciling: "COLLIER COMPANY PURE WHITE LEAD, BLEACHED, St. Louis."

Mauls: Six to eight pound mauls, packed 12 to the case. Consignee: Vivian and Simpson, Virginia City.

Nails: A wide variety of lengths and manufacture of cut nails were recovered; 35 lots total (fig. 72). They were packed in kegs, approximately 100 pounds each. The speci-mens range from one inch in length to spikes of nearly four inches. The kegs were extremely difficult to recover intact, and it was generally necessary to separate the contents from

Figure 71.   Brass powder flask after treatment in the laboratory.

the kegs. Consignees: Worden and Co., Hell Gate; Stuart and Co., Deer Lodge. Manufacturer's stenciling: "GRUFF BENN--- & CO., CLINTON, OHIO."

Steel Bar Stock: Recovered in the bow; ranging in length from 6 to 10 feet. The round stock is approximately 1/2 inch in diameter; the square and rectangular stock from 1/2 to 1 inch along a side. Weight approximately 600 pounds.

Tar Paper: Approximately 500 pounds of tar paper was encountered in the clay. It appeared to be shipped in 5- by 6-foot sheets, but was not recoverable intact. Specimens were taken for the lab.

PERSONAL POSSESSIONS

Robert Campbell: A box containing girls' clothing, spools of thread, hair brushes, bolts of cloth, two leather book covers, a chalk board, shoes, and handkerchiefs. Consignee: "TO ROBT. CAMPBELL, FT. BENTON."

Atchison Family: A box containing womens' shoes, children's gloves, picture frames, mirrors, wicker sewing basket, a blue dressing gown, almonds, wall lamps, curtains, toys, including small blocks and horse-pulled cart. Consignee: "TO ATCHISON, VIRGINIA CITY, M.T."

Unidentified: A box containing woman's clothing, slippers, a small box of almonds and what appeared to be watermelon seeds, and a Chinese dress in a small, lacquered box with Chinese characters brushed on the lid. Consignee: unknown.

MISCELLANEOUS CARGO

Bull Whips: Fragments of leather bull whips packed with hardware.

Coal: Bituminous; recovered on deck, extreme starboard stern (at transom) near the engineer's or blacksmith's working area. Approximately 500 pounds of the material appeared to be on board at the time of sinking.

Gunpowder: Contained in 1-pound cans, 24 cans to the case. Consignee: Vivian and Simpson, Virginia City.

Howitzer Ammunition: Cannon shot (two types); one contained cannister, the other a 12-pound, exploding ball with timing fuse (fig. 73). Arsenal's stenciling: "CANNON SHELLS FOR MOUNTAIN HOWITZER, 1 doz. SHELLS FIXED FEBR. 1865, 18 FRICTION PRIMERS FROM ST.

LOUIS ARSENAL." The spherical case projectiles contain 82 lead musket balls, .69 inches in diameter, sulphur, and a burster charge of 4 1/2 ounces of No. 2 musket powder. The projectile was fixed with a Borman time fuse and each loaded case is strapped to a conical wooden sabot. According to Switzer (Ms.) the ammunition conforms to the specifications set forth in the *United States Ordnance Manual of 1862.* The other type of mountain howitzer ammunition, cannister shot, conforms closely to the *Ordnance Manual* specifications for the "shrapnel" variety. The sheet tin cylinder was filled with four tiers of musket balls, .69 inches in diameter, packed in sawdust. Friction primers packed in each case of ammunition are standard for the period (*ibid.,* p. 7).

Lead Shot: Approximately 35 pounds of bird shot (approximately No. 7 in size) were recovered on the hull floor. No evidence of containers.

Pipes, Smoking: Several types and sizes recovered; briars and clay; one lot included clay bowls exclusively, others contained stems and bowls. Consignee: Vivian and Simpson, Virginia City. Manufacturer's stenciling: "THE CELEBRATED VIRGINIA POHATAN (CLAY), J. R. FRANKLIN & CO., SOLE AGENTS FOR THE MANUFACTURERS, PAMPLINS DEPOT, APPOMATTOX COUNTY, VA."

Figure 72.   Square-cut nails and wood screws.

Figure 73. Howitzer ammunition; 12-pounder, 4.52 inches in diameter; fixed with Borman fuse.

Rope: A number of rope fragments and evidence of ship's lines were encountered on deck and in the holds. Most were badly deteriorated, and only a few specimens (coiled bunches) were recovered.

Shoe Repair Supplies: Shipped in one box. Included are shoe tops, shoe nails, heels, awls, bits, tin plate, tape measure.

Tobacco: Various types shipped including cigars, plug cut, shredded, ground; all ground varieties were contained in fancy, mitered boxes of walnut. Consignees: Stuart and Co., Deer Lodge; Vivian and Simpson, Virginia City; Worden and Co., Hell Gate. Manufacturers' stenciling: 1) "LADY F-----CIGARS," 2) "KILLICKING SMOKING TOBACCO FROM ---KENS & CO., JAMES PINKHAM, ST. LOUIS, PACKED MARCH, 1865." 3) "SMOKING TOBACCO 1 lb bales, M. S. MEEHAM BROS., ST. LOUIS," 4) "CIGARS J. U. D. Y. HABANA," and 5) "EXTRA FINE MISSOURI WEED, Parksville, Mo."

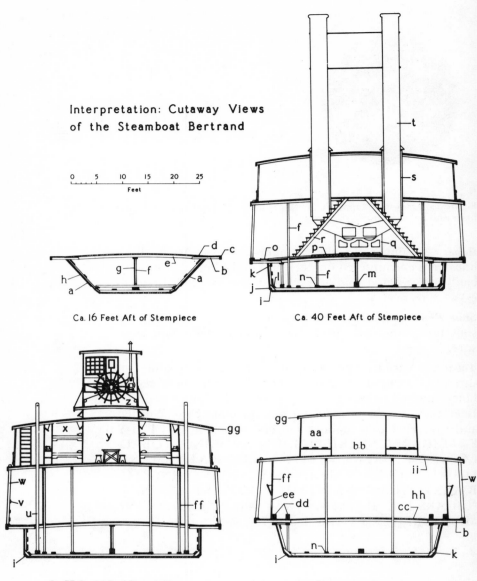

Interpretation: Cutaway Views
of the Steamboat Bertrand

Ca. 16 Feet Aft of Stempiece

Ca. 40 Feet Aft of Stempiece

Ca. 75 Feet Aft of Stempiece

Ca. 163 Feet Aft of Stempiece

Figure 74. Interpretive sectional views of the *Bertrand* at selected distances aft of the stempiece. a. ice shield, b. outriggers, c. guard, d. main deck, e. deck beams, f. stanchions, g. bulkheads, h. side planking, i. knuckle, j. cocked hat (futtock), k. top wale strake (clamp), l. bilge keelson, m. main (central) keelson, n. floor strake, o. ash trap door, p. ash trough and fire brick, q. firebox and boilers, r. stairway to boiler deck, s. heat jacket, t. stacks, u. hog chain brace, v. rails, w. stationaries, x. berths, y. dining area and kitchen, z. pilot house, aa. tiolets, bb. boiler deck, cc. main deck, dd. cylinder timbers, ee. engine room ventilators, ff. bulkheads, gg. cabin roof, hh. engine room, ii. carlines.

PART 5

ARCHITECTURE AND GRAPHIC RECONSTRUCTION

Photographs of the *Bertrand* have not been found, and builders of her day did not work from prepared sets of plans. Nevertheless, a reasonably accurate interpretation of the ship's lines, at least to the top of the boiler deck, can be approximated (figs. 74, 75). In general, the *Bertrand* can be characterized as an upper Ohio River stern wheeler, a packet built for shallow water and constructed for the express purpose of negotiating up-river environments.

Careful recording of the position of stationaries and stanchions, some remains of which were observed protruding through the main deck, suggests the extent of the boiler deck which supported the passengers' and officers' cabins. The presence or absence of a texas deck may never be known and, lacking such evidence, none is included in graphic interpretations. On the other hand, the system of hog chaining depicted on the drawings rests upon reasonably firm evidence. In several cases the chain ends and butt ends of the hog chain braces or struts were charted in position and recovered, and their angles of cant were measured and recorded. Positions of the stacks and boilers, all removed by early day salvors, were based upon the location of the ash trough, hand pump, and mud and steam drums. Depiction of the location and size of the pilot house, toilets in the stern, and yawl and steam fittings were all based upon photographs of boats similar to those of the *Bertrand's* class and manufacture.

THE HULL

With the exception of the bow sides and forecastle, which had been chopped away by early salvors (fig. 1), the hull was found virtually intact, although badly contorted. The major structural members, including the sides and bottom planking, keelsons, ribs,

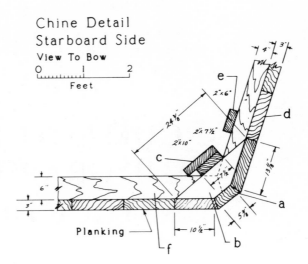

Chine Detail
Starboard Side
View To Bow

Figure 76. Section of chine, starboard side, approximately 8 feet forward of transom; view to bow; a. knuckle, b. cocked hat or futtock, c. bilge keelson, d. side planking, e. strake, f. bottom rib.

footlines, yokes, spar chain straps, cylinder timbers, boiler supporting beams, kevels, strakes, outriggers, and deck beams, were all constructed of white oak, rough sawn and held in place by common bolts and a few square cut nails. The main decking, guard planking, and hatch framing and covers were of white pine, nailed in place and caulked with pitch and oakum.

The hull was carvel-built, bottom and side planks meeting flush at the seams, the construction beginning with bottom planking varying in thickness of from 2 1/2 to 3 inches. The central keelson, from stem to stern, was built up of four layers of overlapping oak beams.[1] The chines were then set (fig. 76), the cylinder timbers and hog chain braces installed, followed by side ribs and planking, stringers and their supports, the bulkheads, transom, outriggers and guard, and finally the main deck. The side and bottom planking and interior supporting strakes were scarf-jointed at intervals which appear to have been simply the length of available lumber (fig. 75).

The dead flat area, i.e., the mid-portion of the hull where water and buttock lines are straight and the bottom flat, appears to have involved nearly one-third of the length of the boat amidships, with the bow and stern sheers involving one-third each of the remaining length (fig. 77). This development, contributing in part to the general trend of decreasing the depth of hold in order to sustain add-

---

[1]Dimensions of the major structural members of the hull appear in Appendix C, "A Study to Determine Volume, Weight, and Density of the Hull of the *Bertrand.*"

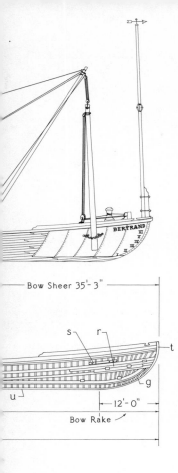

Bow Sheer 35'- 3"

s   r

t

g

u

12'- 0"

Bow Rake

ns,
rse).

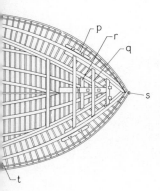

p
r
q

s

t

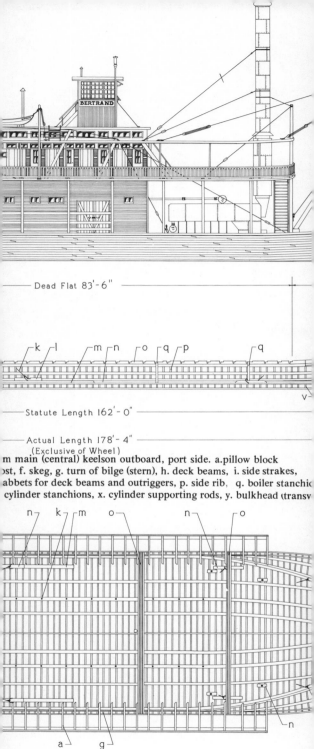

— Dead Flat 83'-6" —

k   l   m n   o q   p   q

— Statute Length 162'-0" —

— Actual Length 178'-4" —
(Exclusive of Wheel)

m main (central) keelson outboard, port side. a.pillow block
ost, f. skeg, g. turn of bilge (stern), h. deck beams, i. side strakes,
abbets for deck beams and outriggers, p. side rib, q. boiler stanchi
cylinder stanchions, x. cylinder supporting rods, y. bulkhead (transv

n   k   m   o   n   o

a   g

0   5   10   15   20 Feet

b. wing (slave) rudder, c. guard, d. hog chain, e. cylinder timber
. deck stanchion positions, l. main keelson, m. side keelson, n.
y, s. stempiece, t. hog chains, u. cylinder cradles, v. rudder stops.

Figure 75. Interpretation of the Bertrand lines.

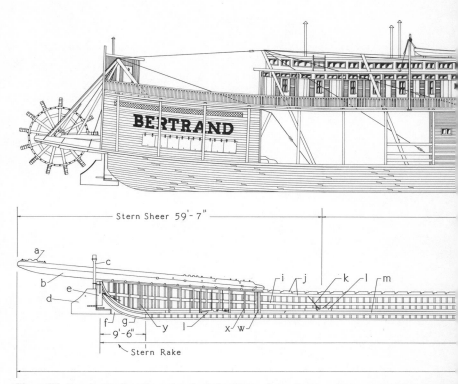

Figure 77. Longitudinal section; view depicting sheer of vessel and major structural members fr(
(lower section), b. cylinder timber, c. upper rudder assembly, d. balance (master) rudder, e. stern p
j. top wale strakes (clamp), k. hog chains, l. footlings, m. side keelson, n. main (central) keelson, o.
r. yoke assembly, s. spar chain strap (interior), t, stempiece, u. bottom planking, v. bottom ribs, w

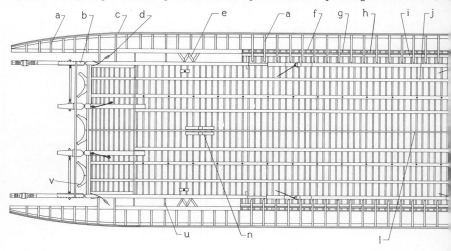

Figure 78. Plan of hull bottom; all decking and remnants of superstructure removed. a. outriggers,
brace, f. side planking, g. side ribs, h. top wale strake (clamp), i, bilge keelson, j. floor strakes, l
footling, o. boiler beams, p. spar chain strap (interior), q. upper yoke assembly, r. lower yoke assemb

ed weight with less draft, was well underway by the mid-19th century, and was typical of steamboats on western rivers (Hunter, 1949 p. 73; Bates, 1968, fig. 29). The depth of the hold, measured in the dead flat area from the top of the bottom planking to the underside of the deck beams, is 5 feet, 2 inches, precisely the measurement recorded on the certificate of enrollment.[2] The width of hold measured from the port to starboard inside planking at deck level is 32 1/2 feet, 3 inches less than that recorded in the enrollment record. Statute length, measured from stempiece to sternpost abutting the transom, is 162 feet, slightly greater than the recorded enrollment of 161 feet. These discrepancies may be the result of the contortions the hull has undergone as a result of settling and the pressure of the surrounding soil, or the difficulty in obtaining precise field measurements of the warped hull when it was exposed during the summer of 1969. At any rate, the differences between field measurements and the enrollment record are so minor as to constitute still further evidence that the remains of the boat excavated is actually that of the *Bertrand*.

Running nearly the entire length of the hull, from the transverse bulkhead to the upper bow yoke, is the remains of a single longitudinal bulkhead separating the hold in halves (frontispiece, figs. 1, 78). Both the longitudinal and transverse bulkheads, the latter separating the hold area from the stern bilge, were constructed of white pine and extended vertically, approximately 5 to 6 inches higher than the sides, thus resulting in a crowned main deck to afford drainage. Upon excavation, the guards appeared to extend horizontally and are so depicted in figure 74, although the guards of many riverboats of the period exhibited a slight insloping, i.e., upward cant (Bates 1968, p. 23).

The *Bertrand* appears to have had at least five hatches on the main deck leading to the holds in the hull. A single stern bilge hatch, approximately 2 1/2 by 3 feet, was encountered early in the excavation period of 1968 (figs. 24, 29). Near this hatch was a square opening which had been cut into the main deck by early-day salvors. Three-quarter-inch holes had been drilled into the decking and a portion of the hatch cover at approximately 5-inch intervals; the boards were then sawed and torn away, allowing access to the bilge. While it is uncertain whether the bilge was used to carry cargo, none was recovered in the area by the salvors of 1968-69. Two main loading hatches were situated 38 feet forward of the transom and were found with hatch covers removed. The remains of two forward hatches were found approximately 33 feet to the rear of the stempiece. The latter

---

[2]Record Group 41, Records of the Bureau of Marine Inspection and Navigation, General Services Administration, National Archives and Record Service, Washington D.C.

four hatches appear to have provided the major access to the holds and were unobstructed by superstructure.

Among the more striking features of the hull were the cylinder timbers, large oaken beams attached to the hull with wooden stanchions and 1-inch vertical iron rods. The four timbers supporting the cylinders, a pair on either side, were actually composite pieces of several beams and were so attached to the hull as to allow some forward and backward play as the linear motion of the pitman was converted to the circular motion at the shaft (figs. 77-79). The long cylinder timbers, which supported the engine cylinder and paddle wheel bearing, were allowed to move slightly upon piston thrusting to absorb shock, accomplished primarily by the flexible iron rods running from the bottom of the timbers to the hull. The cylinders, pistons, and most of the other driving mechanism had been removed by earlier salvors. The distance between each of the timbers in the pairs was 1 foot, 9 inches, which would have allowed at least 18-inch cylinders lying in cradles crossing each pair of beams.

Figure 79.   Top view of wooden kevel at port quarter (top center of photograph). Note also top view of the pair of cylinder timbers below the kevel; a. inner timber, b. outer timber, c. kevel.

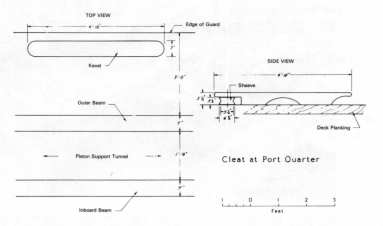

TOP VIEW

Edge of Guard

Kevel

Outer Beam

Piston Support Tunnel

Inboard Beam

SIDE VIEW

Sheave

Deck Planking

Cleat at Port Quarter

0   1   2   3
Feet

Figure 80. Rendering of kevel, situated on guard at sternmost port quarter.

Other hull features of note included two kevels (wooden cleats with steel sheaves) at the port and starboard stern quarters, situated on the guards, and used for tie down (figs. 79, 80). Similar kevels were probably installed at the bow, although no evidence remained after the activities of the early salvors, which included the chopping and tearing away of the forecastle.

The reconstruction drawing (fig. 75) depicts the *Bertrand* equipped for grasshoppering, a spar and pulley arrangement which allowed the boat to be levered across sandbars. The spar straps were still intact in the bow and the remains of the chains were briefly exposed during the excavation period of 1969.

Note should also be made of the heavy beam supporting system, a pair of yokes, in the bow (figs. 78, 81). These yokes, used to support the powered capstan and timberhead, and to provide additional strength to the bow, were heavy oak timbers attached to the strakes and keelsons. As with other portions of the driving mechanism, the capstan had long ago been salvaged, although its horizontal shaft and gear still lay in pillow blocks attached to the longitudinal bulkhead near the bow.

Considered as a unit, the hull conformed to the ideals of the time for shallow draft boats designed for upper river navigation. The vessel's riblines and waterlines (fig. 82), drawn at the time the hull was exposed, are indicative of the simple construction of such craft. The *Bertrand's* hull was flexible, a necessary feature for successful negotiation of sandbars and other low-water hazards. Even as it settled to the bottom upon sinking and after the salvaging of the hog chain trussing system, its severe bowing amidships resulted in few splits or

Figure 81. Yoke assembly in the extreme portion of bow. The two notches cut into the crosspiece of this upper yoke assembly are set to receive the timberhead which extended through the deck. Note also the frayed tops of the side ribs which had been chopped and snapped off in early salvage attempts.

breaks of major supporting members. That it weakened the structure considerably there is no doubt, but the tractable nature of the wood was such that it "gave" readily. The *Bertrand's* straight-sided or model bow, quite unlike the spoonbill types that were just beginning to be constructed for the upper Missouri packets, was typical of those built in the Pittsburgh area in the 1860's. The use of substantial amounts of lightweight white pine—all decking and much superstructure—and the slight framing and light scantling were employed to decrease draft by the builders of the *Bertrand* and others similar to her manufacture (Sweeney, 1887, pp. 649-650). As one steamboat authority described such construction, the hulls were built by rule of thumb and "with all the lightness in any way consistent with safety against falling to pieces" (Hunter, 1949, p. 81).

Evidence of several architectural lines of descent is readily apparent in the hull, including early ocean going steamships, but by the time the *Bertrand* was built, certain characteristics of flatboats and "broadhorns" with dimunitive keels (or none at all) and slight hull modeling had long been employed by Wheeling and Pittsburgh boatwrights. The topheavy, boxlike superstructures of the mid-19th century were already reduced in size and height for western steamers, and the *Bertrand* certainly exemplifies such developments. On the other hand, the marked sheer of ocean going craft, *i.e.*, the rise in the deck, fore and aft of amidships, was built into the hull and persisted for several years into the 1870's. Certain modifications adopted for western river steamers, such as the spoonbill bow, and the long forward rake of the bow to enable the craft to make easy landings, were not made for the *Bertrand*. But the major developments of the 1850's and 1860's, which resulted in the light hulls with shallow draft, facilitated primarily by hog chain systems and the use of a good deal of metal trussing, were incorporated in the *Bertrand*, thus making her quite adaptable for upper-river navigation on most waterways in the United States.

PADDLE WHEEL AND RUDDERS

Although the paddle wheel had been removed from its pillow blocks at the ends of the cylinder timbers, three spare flanges (fig. 30), and a single arm (fig. 32) were found on the main deck—portions that allow a reasonable graphic reconstruction of the paddle wheel

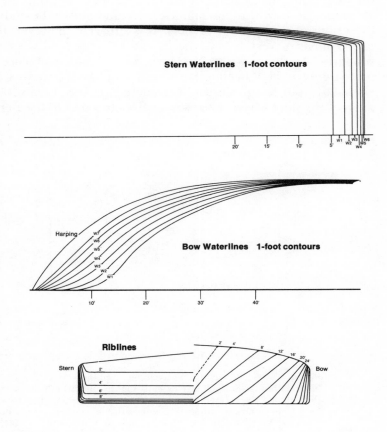

Figure 82. The *Bertrand's* waterlines and riblines.

itself. The stern wheel was equipped with 13 arms and buckets attached to flanges, the latter of which could be separated in halves for easy replacement. The wheel shaft on the boat was round, in contrast to the usual hexagonal shape, and a series of keys kept the flanges from turning on the shaft. Based on the radial distance from the center of the pillow block to a point approximately 4 inches short of the stern arc of the rudder, the paddle wheel appears to have been about 18 feet in diameter. Allowing 4 inches of clearance on both sides of the wheel and the outer cylinder timber and the side of the pillow block, the wheel would have been about 28 feet long.

It is of more than ordinary interest that the *Bertrand's* stern paddle wheel and support system were typical of those which had reached a peak of development for western packets a few years later. For many years, the stern wheels were supported within the lines of the hull rather than extending beyond the hull as in the case of the *Bertrand*, i.e., revolving on pillow blocks mounted at the ends of the extensions of the cylinder timbers. It is apparent, however, that the employment of very heavy wheels, extending beyond the hull and supported by their own truss system, was already a practice of the boatwrights in the Wheeling-Pittsburgh area by 1865. It must be noted that the four features usually considered to exemplify full development of the stern wheel systems were already a part of the *Bertrand's*

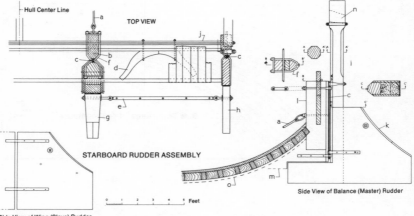

Figure 83. Starboard rudder assembly, top and side views. The balance (master) rudder on each side extends slightly under both the stern rake of the hull and the former position of the paddle wheel; a. hog chain and its heel, b. stern post, c. pintle, d. rudder stops, e. rudder articulating arm, f. hinges, g. lower (balance) rudder assembly, h. wing (slave) rudder, i. upper (balance) rudder assembly, j. false transom, k. wheel arc, l. stern post, m. skeg, n. tiller bar socket, o. stern rake.

Figure 84. Top view of rudder assembly, starboard side. Note the articulating arm connecting the master and slave rudders which are jammed against the 90-degree stops.

design by 1864, notably: 1) removal of the wheel from the stern recess, 2) the use of a pair of pistons driving the wheel at opposite ends of the shaft, 3) the incorporation of the wheel assembly with the hogchain trussing system, and 4) the use of multiple balance rudders (Hunter, 1949, pp. 172, 173). Considering these features alone, the *Bertrand* would appear to have been a reflection of the latest thinking in the design and construction of upper-river steamers.

Unfortunately, detailed features of the paddle wheel must remain conjectural. It is known, for example, that some boats of the 1850's and 1860's incorporated wheels which compensated for the weight of the crank with selectively weighted buckets, thereby obtaining a smoother flow of power. Another important refinement of the time was the division of the buckets in halves, and setting one set half a space in advance of those on the other side (Wallace, 1865, pp. 102, 103; for an excellent sketch see Bates, 1968, p. 95, fig. 135). While these features may well have been a part of the wheel, evidence is lacking and they are not depicted in the graphic reconstructions.

The rudder assembly of the *Bertrand* also appears to have been quite sophisticated for mid-19th century, shallow water boats. Two master rudders, each articulated with a slave, extend under the paddle wheel and stern rake of the hull (figs. 83, 84). The rudder system is clearly an example of an evolutionary process in which single rudders eventually gave way to two, three, and even four articulated rudders (Russell, 1961, p. 106). The rudders were hinged to the stern posts and skegs which, in turn, were attached to the transom and hull bottom. Fragments of a false transom were also observed aft of the vertical rudder assembly.

As with many riverboats of the period, the *Bertrand* was equipped with a pair of skegs forward of the master rudders, devices which tended to prevent side slip and to reduce accumulation of drift. Regrettably, exact measurements of the skegs and their method of attachment to the turn of the bilge could not be determined inasmuch as the salvors did not expose those portions of the stern.[3]

HOG CHAIN TRUSS SYSTEM

The marked increase of the length-to-breadth ratio which was employed by builders of almost all western steamers at the time the *Bertrand* was constructed necessitated a rather complex longitudinal truss system of iron rods (hog chains) and braces to support the relatively heavy ends of the boat. In the case of the *Bertrand* and other stern wheelers of her size, the braces extended from the keelsons to a point slightly above the superstructure. While only fragments of the hog chain system remained in the hull and on the main deck, the appearance and positions of the major elements can be reconstructed with reasonable accuracy.

Long a central problem in the construction of lightly built riverboats, means of adding longitudinal or girder strength to prevent hogging and sagging eventually resulted in a system of long wooden braces and iron rods which could be tightened or loosened by turnbuckles (fig. 85). Braces employed in the system were usually firmly attached to keelsons or other heavy members and extended through the boiler deck. Both the remains of the bracing timbers and the opening in the main deck through which they protruded were carefully mapped as the sand and mud was cleared. The bottom angles of the braces were recorded, allowing the artist to project their cant above the main deck. Their lengths were based upon photographs of other boats of the same general class as the *Bertrand*. Positions of the ends of tie rods and hog chains were also mapped for the beam and truss arrangement of the paddle wheel, and the entire scheme is depicted along with the reconstruction of the superstructure in figure 75.

ENGINE REMAINS

Very few parts of the engines were found during the excavation period of 1969. The early day salvors apparently had been quite

---

[3]Although the salvors had no plans to excavate anywhere outside the periphery of the holds, upon the author's request they did expose enough of the stern area to measure the rudders and a slight portion of the stern rake. Further excavation in the area, without elaborate buttressing, was considered dangerous, both to personnel and to the structure itself.

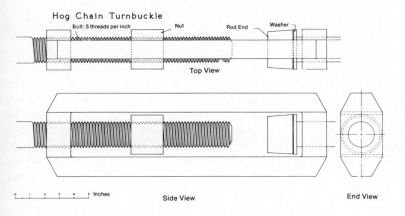

Figure 85.   Detail of typical turnbuckle used to tighten hog chains.

successful in removing nearly everything of value or, at any rate, everything that could be used again in the construction of other boats or
to power sawmills, as was often the practice following the sinking and
recovery of riverboats on the Missouri. The literature on the subject
of salvaging sunken steam vessels in the west is full of references to
the activity of divers primarily intent on recovering the engine parts,
cylinders, pistons, boilers, and camshaft assemblies in particular (King
1863:182, 183; *cf. Sen. Ex. Doc. 42, 32nd Cong., I Sess.*, p. 110).

Evidence seems clear that the engines and possibly other
parts were originally installed in another vessel. Earl Chapin May, in
his *Principio to Wheeling* (New York, 1945) relates the activities of a
number of steamboat builders and fitters of Wheeling, and in his discussion of A. J. Sweeney, the installer of the Bertrand engines, reports the following:

> Wheeling's river traffic developed many legendary figures. There
> was a Captain A. J. Sweeney, of the North Wheeling shipyards,
> who built a steamboat bearing his name for Captain George Hill of
> St. Louis, and which finished her long career on the Cumberland
> River by colliding with a pier at Nashville. Although they raised her
> machinery, brought it back to Wheeling and installed it in the *Ber-
> traut* [sic], that boat sank in the Missouri River and became a total
> loss. (May, 1945, p. 159)

There is no record of a steamer *Bertraut* on the Missouri,
and it appears that the name was either misspelled or misprinted.
Efforts at tracing the route of the engines after they were salvaged by
the insuror's divers were made without success.

Despite the activity of the early salvors, those remaining parts that were recovered on the deck during the summer of 1969, and the positions of the auxiliary features associated with the engines, do allow general statements as to their conformity and design. The coursed firebrick, ask trough, and mud and steam drums on the main deck immediately to the rear of the forecastle clearly indicate the former location of the boilers (fig. 29). During the period when the *Bertrand* was constructed, the boilers were built over the mud drum and below the steam drum, and were fueled and stoked from the bow where cords of wood were loaded and stored for immediate use. While we can be reasonably certain that the boilers were positioned horizontally, judging from the location of the long ash trough which terminated at the starboard guard trap door, details of construction such as thickness of plate, length and breadth of boiler, and flue arrangements may never be known. By the 1870's, however, most non-condensing, high pressure engines for western boats constructed in the Pittsburgh area were served by long, cylindrical boilers with a pair of internal flues, and with the firebox at the bow end (Hodge, 1840; Wallace, 1865, pp. 103-109).

The cylinders, one on either side of the boat, were firmly attached to the cylinder supporting beams. Unfortunately, we can rely on only a very few sketches and photographs of engines constructed as early as 1864. However, the *Bertrand's* driving mechanism must certainly have been quite similar to the classic horizontal example depicted by Paul R. Hodge in 1840 (see also Hunter, 1949, p. 140, and Tredgold, 1851, vol. II, pt. I). We can, for example, be reasonably certain that the valve and cam system employed on the *Bertrand* included an adjustable eccentric, i.e., cutoff, mounted on the shaft of the paddle wheel which allowed the engineer to close the steam valve at any desired point in the stroke (Wallace, 1865, pp. 142-144). This allowed the use of a full stroke cam to be employed when the boat was getting underway and whenever maximum power was required, and of the adjustable cutoff, allowing economical use of steam pressure under ordinary conditions. Both types of cams were found in the excavation, either spares or the original equipment overlooked by the early salvors. The halves of the full stroke and exhaust cams are depicted in figure 31.

GRAPHIC RECONSTRUCTION

As has been noted, the graphic reconstruction of the lines of the *Bertrand* was accomplished in large measure by projecting the remains and fragments of features which survived the activity of early salvors, and by the use of photographs of boats known to have been

constructed in a very similar manner. Beginning with the scale drawings and photographs of the hull itself, such vertical members as stanchions extending to the bottom of the boiler deck and the braces running at various angles from the keelsons were drawn in place, positioned on the basis of their stumps, or the holes in the main deck
through which they passed. The survival of a single whole stanchion
or stationary which was found lying on the deck allowed us to determine accurately the height of the boiler deck from the main deck.

The extension of the boiler deck forward was readily determined by the limits of the stanchion sockets and openings in the main
deck through which the stanchions passed. It was found that the boiler deck ended just forward of the stacks, which would have allowed
reasonably easy access to the forward hatches. The positions of the
stacks and boilers, as previously noted, were based upon the location
of the bottom of the firebox and ash trough.

Sidings (bulkheads) projecting from the main deck were
held in place, at least in part, by quarter-round molding which was
mapped in place before decking was removed and thereby the periphery of the areas enclosed on the main deck could be determined
with some confidence. Thus, the graphic reconstruction of the *Bertrand*, at least to the level of the boiler deck, proceeded by simple extension of features known to have been a part of the steamer, and a
very general description of her appearance to this point involves few
problems. From this point, however, one must proceed with much
less assurance by relying upon a number of published sources and
photographs of steamers known to have been similar in design. The
cabin area above the boiler deck in the stern was drawn somewhat

Interpretation: Bertrand Boiler Deck and Cabins

0   5   10   15   20   Feet

short of the full length of the boiler deck itself, a characteristic of steamers built for the upper Ohio River trade. The fact that the *Bertrand* was a packet, *i.e.*, carrying both passengers as well as freight, would have required that she be able to house a number of persons in reasonable comfort, in addition to the officers. It is assumed that there were at least four crew members on board who would have been housed in quarters separate from other crew members, including the captain, clerk, and two engineers. In addition, such craft normally carried a chambermaid' and cook, who were sometimes housed in the cabin area but were not given staterooms when packets were carrying a full passenger complement. While we cannot be certain of the number of first class passengers on board, one newspaper account mentions the figure of 20 (*Sunday Journal and Star*, April 12, 1936). Therefore, the number and size of cabins depicted in figure 86 was not considered unreasonable.[4] Such considerations as the exact positions of the pilot house, dories and their supporting davits, etc., were necessarily based upon photographs of similar craft.

Two photographs of contemporary steam vessels were particularly helpful in the graphic reconstruction of certain details of the superstructure, namely the *Deer Lodge* (fig.87), and the *Lida Norvell* (fig. 88). The *Bertrand's* cabin was built at Pittsburgh at about the same time as that of the *Deer Lodge* (Way, 1950, p.8), a packet which ran ahead of the *Bertrand* several days, also enroute to Fort Benton. The *Deer Lodge*, with a spoonbill bow, but with superstructure characteristic of the upper Ohio River packets, is very likely to have shared certain features with the *Bertrand*, particularly the main stairs running athwartship, the cabin roof extending forward somewhat beyond the cabin itself, the presence of cabin skylights, stanchions, bull rails, and a full boiler deck.

The only surviving photograph of the *Lida Norvell* is a poor one—an enlargement made from a photograph of a number of boats. She was constructed in 1865 at Portsmouth, Ohio, was used in trade on the Yazoo, Red and Yalobusha Rivers, measured only 88 tons, and was 103 feet in length (Lytle, 1952, p. 112), considerably smaller than the *Bertrand*. This craft was a very typical packet operating in the Ohio area. It was constructed with a model bow, guards, overhanging boiler deck, enclosed engine room, and with no texas—all traits it most likely shared with the *Bertrand*.

Perhaps the major point of contention and conjecture regarding the appearance of the superstructure of the *Bertrand* in-

---

[4]Figure 86 was prepared following the suggestions and advice of Alan L. Bates, architect and steamboat authority. The drawing is conjectural, but is representative of the cabin arrangements of Upper Ohio river packets of the time of the *Bertrand's* manufacture.

Figure 87. The *Deer Lodge*, ca. 1865, constructed to the specifications of the owners of the *Bertrand*, shared many traits of the latter. (Photo courtesy of Alan R. Bates, Louisville, Ky.)

Figure 88. The only known photograph of the *Lida Norvell*, taken in the summer of 1865 at Cincinnati. This upper Ohio River vessel, while somewhat smaller than the *Bertrand*, appears to have shared with her most of the outward characteristics. Compare the photograph with figure 75, the graphic reconstruction of the *Bertrand's* lines. (Photo courtesy of the Cincinnati Public Library.)

volves the question of whether the boiler deck supported by stationaries extended to a point nearly directly over the edge of the guards below. Two persistent characteristics of boats built specifically for the upper Missouri trade was the lack of guards and the shaping of the bow into a "spoonbill" form such as that of the *Deer Lodge,* which Copelin and Roe had constructed especially for their business between St. Louis and Fort Benton. The *Bertrand* did have guards and a straight-sided, upper Ohio River bow. Very limited portions of the guards were exposed during the excavation, and those portions which were exposed were helpful in determining the dimensions and limits of the guards and the interval distances of supporting outriggers, but did not reveal sockets or evidence of the former existence of stationaries. However, all other evidence seems to point to the *Bertrand* as having been designed for upper Ohio River work and, therefore, the graphic reconstructions include stationaries and an overhanging boiler deck (fig. 74). If or when the hull is again exposed and careful examination of the periphery of the guards is made, it may be found that stationaries were once positioned along the edges.

Unfortunately, we have no historical description of the *Bertrand* such as that which is available for the *Deer Lodge,* a steamer which shared so many characteristics. The similarities of the vessels appear remarkable as one reviews the comment of General Phillippe Regis de Trobriand, who was a passenger on the *Deer Lodge* in 1867:

> The general construction is simple. The hull is flat, almost without a keel, made to displace as little water as possible. When completely loaded, it does not draw more than 4 feet of water, average 3 to 3 1/2 ft. Under the first deck, the hull forms the hold where the merchandise is stacked one half to two thirds the length of the boat, the forward deck is open. The stern is closed in a room to protect the engines and serves as a repair shop. The furnaces and boilers are on the deck, forward of the engines. They pile firewood port, starboard, and forward, leaving a passage for the crew on each side of it. In front of the furnaces, there is an open stairway which leads up to the Upper Deck. This deck supported the length of the boat by castiron columns, encloses a dining room or salon in the center, from which all cabins open on port and starboard. . .Outside the cabins on both sides there is a gallery onto which each cabin opens by a glass door. The great paddle board wheel which propels her is as wide as the stern. The pilot house, which contains the wheel is located on the upper deck between two high smokestacks and a little astern. She was armed with a field piece and carried both a carpenter and a blacksmith. (Kane, 1951, pp. 24-25)

During that period of time when attempts were being made to reconstruct graphically the lines of the *Bertrand* from those ship's parts and fittings that survived, several authorities on the architecture of the western steamboat were consulted by the author. These men reviewed the initial field drawings, photographs and maps made at the time of excavation, submitted reports, and corresponded at some length in their deliberations. Their comments excerpted below contain pertinent information on the boat and provide alternative interpretations of structure and history. Their recommendations for changes in the initial graphic reconstruction were followed, and were incorporated in the figures included in this work.

THE PROBABLE APPEARANCE
OF THE STEAMER BERTRAND

by Alan L. Bates[5]

The aim of this report is to give a general idea of the arrangement and appearance of the steamer *Bertrand*. In the last paragraph of most such reports it is admitted that they are of limited value. This one is different: it states so from the start for, unless and until a contemporary photograph of the *Bertrand* is discovered somewhere, certain aspects of her appearance shall always remain conjectural.

There is a limited amount of data available on this vessel. Most important are accurate drawings prepared from measurements when her hull was exposed, particularly the cabin support members at the main deck level (fig. 29). Enrollment papers list her hull dimensions and nominal tonnage capacity. Newspaper accounts indicate that she was a very light boat, drawing but 18 inches when empty, with a plain and unadorned cabin. The accuracy of newspapers is always open to a serious doubt, however, due to reportorial ignorance, inflated hometown pride, and, frequently, outright lying on the part of interviewees.

There is much data available about similar contemporary vessels in the forms given above and also in photographic recording. A clear photograph of the steamer *Deer Lodge* is in existence (fig. 87), (Way, 1950, p. 83). It is important for this report because the *Deer Lodge's* cabin was built at the same time and place as that of the *Bertrand*, albeit specifically for the Fort Benton trade. The *Deer Lodge* was very nearly the same size as the *Bertrand*, i.e., 4 feet longer, 3 feet wider, and the same depth. Both vessels were smaller than those used on other rivers in long distance trades.

The *Deer Lodge* was built for the Montana and Idaho Transportation Line, headed by John J. Roe and John Copelin of St. Louis, and, thus, certainly incorporated her owners' desired characteristics previously demonstrated by other successful mountain steam-

[5]Mr. Bates is an architect and author of articles and books dealing with the construction and appearance of riverboats. His best known work is the *Western Rivers Steamboat Cyclopoedium* (Hustle Press, Leonia, N.J., 1968). Mr. Bates served as the mate of the *Belle of Louisville*, and was instrumental in the establishment of the Howard National Steamboat Museum at Jeffersonville, Ind.

ers. The *Bertrand*, however, was built for and owned by persons residing at or near Wheeling, Va. on the upper Ohio River. While there is little doubt that she was intended for use on very shallow waters, there is no real indication that she was built for the extreme conditions of the upper Missouri River. Such boats were used almost universally on the tributaries of the western rivers system and on mainstems during periods of drought (Hunter, 1949, p. 219 *et seq.*). Their adaptation to conditions of navigation on the Missouri was easy. It might be said that the true mountain boat was an evolutionary refinement of these ubiquitous members of the Ohio River "mosquito fleet."

Three possibilities are suggested by available data: 1) the *Bertrand* was an ordinary Ohio River, low-water packet; or 2) she was a Missouri River mountain steamer; or 3) she was a hybrid with an Ohio River packet hull and a mountain steamer cabin. The shape of the bow and the existence of overhanging main deck guards would appear to eliminate the second possibility, for the fully developed mountain steamer had a bowl-like, spoonbill bow and no guards. Neither of these characteristics apply to the *Bertrand*. If the *Bertrand* was built for use on the upper Ohio River she would, characteristically, have guards, stationaries, bull rails, and a fully-roofed boiler deck.

Evidence of her intended use could be inferred from enrollment documents indicating whether she was bought or chartered by the Montana and Idaho Transportation Line. A charter would imply her eventual return to her regular Ohio River trade and, therefore, no significant changes in her superstructure. An outright sale, especially if it were consummated prior to her completion, would imply a Missouri River mountain cabin.

The *Bertrand* was known to have been advertised for her mountain trip several weeks before she was completed in November, 1864 (Jerome E. Petsche, personal communication). This raises the intriguing question of whether she was bought or chartered by the Montana and Idaho Transportation Line prior to her completion. If so, there is a strong possibility that her new owners changed the cabin design after the hull was framed or after it was completed.

One important factor tends to support the position that the *Bertrand* carried stationaries and bull rails. It would be unusual for a packet to stow as much freight in the hull as the archeologists found there unless the main deck was occupied by other freight such as cattle, horses, or deck passengers that could not be carried in the hold. Yet the hold was "chock-a-block" full. The presence of a deckroom is indicated by a pair of quarter-round mouldings attached to the deck. A temporary bulkhead or corral could be slipped between the vertical faces of these moldings which were approximately 1 1/2 inches apart. Men could occupy such a deckroom, while cattle or horses were prevented from walking overboard by the bull rails. Or the reverse could have been the case, where the cattle would be confined within the corral area, and the deck passengers protected by the bull rails. Horses and cattle were certainly in demand in Montana at that time. Additionally, because of the difficulty of preserving fresh meat, a part of the boat's victuals was often carried on the hoof and slaughtered as needed.

Conclusions

Any conclusion regarding the cabin's appearance must necessarily involve a good deal of intuitive reasoning. Despite the tantalizing questions posed above, I believe the *Bertrand* had a typical Ohio River low-water packet cabin with stationaries and bull rails around the main deck. Her cabin was probably short with an open, roofed gangway aft. Her extremely light draft would tend to indicate that there was no texas deck.

If research reveals that the Montana and Idaho Transportation Line did indeed buy the hull and order the cabin to select specification, then a cabin like that of the *Deer Lodge* was almost certainly built. The enclosed portion of the cabin would be very short with the forward promenade unroofed and the after gangway also unroofed. This would be the hybrid possibility described in alternative 3 above.

Following his formal report on the probable appearance of the *Bertrand*, and after reviewing our preliminary architectural line reconstructions, Mr. Bates again wrote the author to suggest further modifications of our interpretations, and to propose a probable cabin arrangement.

I have red-lined your preliminary side view of the *Bertrand* and sketched one possible cabin arrangement (fig. 86) which would have slept 36 passengers. If the open gangway aft were reduced in size and the cabin lengthened, capacity would be increased. I have assumed that there would have been no texas deck, and that the licensed crew would have slept in the forward end of the cabin. The master would have had the forward stateroom on the starboard side, and the clerk with his office would have been quartered opposite. Proceeding aft on the captain's side there would be two engineers, the cook and chambermaid, and four male passengers. Aft of the kitchen and midship gangway would be quartered either family groups or female passengers. If the male passenger population spilled over into this area, they would be given the forward staterooms. The ladies' cabin was always furthest aft. Many river customs and mores were involved here; there was less heat and less immediate danger of flying skyward in the event of boiler explosions. *No* unescorted male ever went into the ladies' portion of the cabin, ever, ever, ever. Aside from being ungallant, there were scandalous overtones in such a *faux pas*. On the best vessels, the gentlemen's cabin was a bare wood deck and the ladies' cabins were carpeted. No gentleman set foot on that carpet without an invita-

tion from a lady, with the exception, or course, of husbands travel-
ling with wives and families.

The kitchen-pantry set-up on my proposed arrangement seems
to be a little wasteful of space. The two rooms could be combined
and additional staterooms located along the port side. Four more
paying passengers could thus be accommodated. The pantry could
be either a serving pantry or a kitchen storage space. It's hard to
say.

The chimneys on your reconstruction should be the same diameter all the way up to their tips and should slope aft about one-
quarter inch per foot of rise. From the roof to below the boiler deck
a heat jacket was placed around the stacks to protect the woodwork
and the crew and passengers.

The laundry and toilet rooms were frequently located as depicted in figure 86. The toilets were open holes leading down through
the deck over the paddlewheel. Much earthy humor grew about
this regarding wheel repairs while people above were attending to
calls of nature. Often the deckhands only stopped the women just a
trifle too late for modesty but in barely enough time to avoid soil-
ing. They merely cursed the men, of course. Dirty laundry water
went through the same way.

The Bertrand would almost certainly have had a jackstaff. No
self-respecting boat of that era was without one. It was useful to the
pilot for gauging distances, heights and, with a windvane at its
peak, the wind direction. A flag was even better since it also provided some idea of wind velocity.

The pilothouse should be set somewhat higher than you have
depicted and the skylight deck under it should be at least 2 feet
higher than the roof to allow the fitting of a row of skylight tran-
soms for the center cabin. I won't quarrel with your yawl location,
for they might have the workboat stored almost anywhere.

Your spars and derricks are properly arranged with the exception of the derricks, which would have some sort of base pocket at
their feet to prevent them from kicking away. This might simply
have been ledge timbers spiked to the deck or a fancy cast pocket
built into the deck. Since the 1865 salvors removed that part of the
deck, we shall never know.

The Deer Lodge is the important photograph included with this
message (fig. 87). This boat ran immediately ahead of the Bertrand
in 1865. She is flying a huge banner with the boat's name appliqued
to it from the jackstaff. That banner is probably 20 feet long and 8
feet tall. Since this boat was built at the same time and place as the
Bertrand, there is much likelihood of similarities in cabin construction. The Deer Lodge's roof is cut off at the after end of the cabin.
Her main stairs run 'thwartship. The boilers were so close to the
front of the superstructure that there was no room for them in the
usual direction. She has stanchions and pockets for bull rails, but
the bull rails are missing except those just forward of the engine

room. They were probably stored in St. Louis. If she were carrying them and had only removed them for unloading freight, those on the riverward side would still be in place. The cabin roof starts somewhat aft of the edge of the boiler deck. Men are standing forward of the roof on the boiler deck. Notice how the hat of the gentleman in black on the right is as high as the roof. The roof was probably seven feet or less above the boiler deck. This boat has no headlight. Can you pick out the chair on the roof forward of the stacks? Good place for the captain or a lookout to perch.

The following letter was written to Alan L. Bates by Captain Frederick Way Jr.[6] following review and study of the field drawings, photographs and historical information on the *Bertrand*.

> 121 River Ave.
> Sewickley, Pa. 15143
> October 26, 1970

Dear Alan,

One should stand off a bit and see the *Bertrand* in historical perspective. She was built in 1864, before the Missouri River type packet was adopted. What we think of as the typical "mountain boat" were those that got going in the early 1870's, probably with the *Far West, E. H. Durfee, Esperanza, Nellie Peck*, etc. Prior to that they were using tramp packets built with rugged hulls acceptable to the Missouri River underwriters. Ergo, the *Bertrand* was built to carry freight, and her commercial success depended on hauling a big tonnage of low class stuff, like pig iron, ore, iron products, and so on. What I'm saying is that packets arriving at Omaha in 1864 were adaptable to the Arkansas, the Cumberland and, yes, even on the Allegheny to Oil City.

The *Deer Lodge* had some definite ideas incorporated into her regarding the Missouri. She came along right after the *Bertrand*. A contemporary news account of the *Deer Lodge* says this of her: "She has no guards on the lower deck, and is built low so as not to catch the wind." The photo seems to substantiate this. The business of having "no guards" could throw anybody for a loss if the picture didn't exist—for she did have stationaries and bull rails.

The *Bertrand* did have guards, almost 4 feet overhang. No evidence seems to exist at the present time whether or not she had stationaries, but my hunch is that she did have them—most tramp

---

[6]Captain Frederick Way, Jr., has had over 30 years of experience working on riverboats, and over 60 years as a historian of rivers and river transportation. He first worked on steamboats in 1918 on Kanawha River packets as a teenager. He holds pilot's and master's licenses, is the author of many books and articles on riverboats, and has one of the largest collections of photographs of North American river craft. His best known works include *The Allegheny* (Rivers of America Series), the *Log of the Betsy Ann*, a number of directories of packets, and the annual series entitled the *Inland River Record*.

packets of that vintage, unless styled for wintering in the south carrying cotton, did have them by 1864.

As to whether *Bertrand* had a texas deck is a puzzle. I don't see any evidence so far one way or the other. I don't believe any news account so far says anything about a texas. Maybe something definite will turn up someday to solve that problem.

To say a few words about the questions you raise on details:

About the two quarter-round strips 64 feet back from the stem: I am not clear as to whether you mean these were thwartship or not, and will venture no opinion. However, the deck plan (fig. 29) shows a heavy black line thwartship at that point, as though a bulkhead is indicated aft the boilers. I cannot conceive of a thwartship bulkhead there. The engineer would have objected strenuously, for one thing.

The half-round thwartship strip between the cylinder timbers makes me wonder whether there was any forward bulkhead to the engine room—apparently not. My guess would be what you suggest, that this was a line marking the engineer's domain, probably to keep the mate from stowing stuff aft of it.

The row of thwartship stanchions 9 feet forward of the transom could very well have been a bulkhead, particularly in view of the possible absence of the one more forward just mentioned. This would have created a "tiller room" so called, housing paint locker, *et al.* I don't think these thwartship stanchions had anything to do with boiler deck doings.

Yes, you've got an orthodox stern set-up; rudders hung on the transom, boxed, and a false transom aft of that, and you can bet your bottom dollar the stern bulkhead thwartship was in line with the aft end of what you call the "cat walk."

The forecastle having been shaved off is something peculiar; I can't see the reasoning here. As you say, it may have been done by the salvors, but looks like a hell of a lot of work to remove a deck.

Hand pumps were common property on boats even in my time, always aft of the boilers, thwartship, used on boiler day. These also doubled as fire pumps and as emergency bilge pumps. A donkey boiler was a luxury on small packets—most of them had none.

I cannot answer with certainty whether steam syphons were in circulation by 1864. Probably yes. But hand pumps were more commonly used.

The trough in lieu of an ashwell was ingenious, and until now I never knew of such a thing.

The evidence of 13 wheel arms will be helpful in establishing the diameter of the paddlewheel by rule-of-thumb. I'm amazed at how the pillow blocks were so far out on the ends of the wheel timbers—how come they didn't use long timbers?

Those extra cabin stanchions at 72 and 104 feet aft of the stempiece don't have anything to do with a texas, I don't think. The weight of freight carried in the cabin would be sufficient reason for them.

My judgement, based on evidence so far established, is that *Bertrand* was a lot like *Deer Lodge*. The cabin deck may have been bobtailed a bit (even on *Deer Lodge* this seems indicated). I'd say no texas unless evidence arrives to the contrary. Cabin skylights, yes. Cabin starts aft of the stack jackets. Big diameter chimneys for her size. A pilothouse a lot wider than it is long. The front steps were divided.

Fred

Drawing upon many years of research on inland water transportation and riverboats, and upon all available historical information on the *Bertrand*, a somewhat different opinion on the appearance of the boat was provided in the following report to the author by Bert Fenn.[7]

The Missouri has been from the beginning, and remains so today, one of the most trying American rivers to navigate. It is shallow, muddy, swift, shifty, snaggy and unpredictable. For these reasons not every western rivers steamboat or even every type of western rivers steamboat was suitable for successful Missouri River use.

The navigable portion of the Missouri River from the mouth to Ft. Benton has been characterized as being composed of two distinct geological sections. From the mouth to Cow Island, more than 2,000 miles, is the "Sandy River" which flows through alluvial soil. The climb from the mouth to Cow Island through this section of Sandy River averages 8.5 inches per mile. This elevation itself presented no great problems; the hazards of the Sandy River were shallowness, the many shifting sandbars, and snags—though these were real enough in themselves.

On the other hand, the final 172 miles from Cow Island to Ft. Benton were entirely different, and this section has been called the "Rocky River" because it cuts through solid rock formations. This is a steep grade averaging 2.07 feet per mile with rapids, loose boulders, and rocky reefs.

There were even more restrictions on the type of boat that could successfully navigate all the way to Ft. Benton, and thus greater care was required in the design or selection of a Ft. Benton boat than for a lower Missouri boat.

The development of a special breed of boat was an evolutionary process of trial and error, not an instantaneous accomplishment. There were no professional marine architects designing western river steamboats in the mid-19th century. The process was to build a boat that seemed to meet the requirements, try her out, improve

---

[7]Mr. Fenn, Tell City, Ind., has conducted historical research on riverboats for over 20 years. He has contributed articles to technical journals, has an extensive file of river photographs, and holds a riverboat master's license. The memorandum was written following a review and study of field drawings and historical information on the *Bertrand* in the archives of the Midwest Archeological Center, National Park Service, Lincoln, Nebr.

her deficiencies, try again, etc. All this took years. And perhaps the only factors that could push the process would have been a demand for many boats and a prospect for quick profits for the right design.

Until the gold boom in Montana there was no great demand for steamboat transportation all the way to Ft. Benton. Indeed, it was not until 1859 that Pierre Chouteau, Jr. built the first boat specifically designed to reach Ft. Benton, the *Chippewa*. The *Chippewa* got within 12 miles of Ft. Benton in 1859 on her first attempt, but it was not until 1860 that she actually reached there. By 1863 when the gold boom was beginning, only six boats had actually reached Ft. Benton. The demand and chance for profit were now present. But there were only a handful of steamboats which had demonstrated their capability of making it all the way to Ft. Benton, and perhaps more significantly, only a handful of pilots who had made the trip and knew the river all the way.

The evolutionary process of developing the ideal Ft. Benton steamboat, the "spoonbill-bow mountain boat" had started. But as Chappell says in *Transaction of the Kansas State Historical Society*, vol. IX p. 293, "There were but few regular boats on the Missouri at that time, but others began to crowd in from every stream west of the Alleghanies, side-wheelers, stern-wheelers, and old tubs." In 1866 there were 31 steamboat arrivals at Ft. Benton.

One characteristic would have been common to all of these steamboats that reached Ft. Benton between 1860 and 1866: they necessarily were shallow boats. But *that* probably was the only characteristic they shared. Some were "low-water boats" from other streams of the Mississippi River system that had been designed and built for those other streams and other trades. Others would be hybrids, trials in the evolutionary process of developing the ideal "spoonbill-bow mountain boat." And these evolutionary boats probably varied a great deal in the early stages.

At this point in my research I cannot pinpoint specifically when the "spoonbill mountain boat" appeared in near typical form. I do not believe it was as early as 1864. I have never seen a photo of a prototype "spoonbill mountain boat" that dates that early. My guess and opinion is that it was nearer to 1870 that the prototype appeared. As I write this I am looking at photos of the following *typical* "spoonbill mountain boats," the *Far West*, built 1870; *E. H. Durfee*, built 1871; *Western*, built 1872; *General Meade*, built 1875; and *F. Y. Batchelor*, built 1878.

These above-named steamers constructed between 1870 and 1878, and other "spoonbill mountain boats" whose photos I have examined, share three characteristics that are not at all typical of low-water boats from other rivers: 1) spoonbill bow, 2) no guards, and 3) they have only one deck, the boiler deck, above the main, with a very small cabin atop this.

On the other hand, low-water boats from another tributary would typically share 1) more of a model bow, 2) guards, 3) uprights and bullrails on the guards and 4) a boiler deck cabin with huricane roof above. If we follow this line of reasoning, there are only two choices as to the appearance of the *Bertrand:* 1) that it was a hybrid in the evolutionary development of the prototype "spoon-bill mountain boat," or 2) that it was a low-water boat designed and built for another river.

It is, after all, who built her and for what use that determined the *Bertrand's* design. What we do know about the *Bertrand:*

a) She was built at Wheeling, W. Va., and her initial owners were two men from Wheeling and three men from Monroe County, Ohio, a neighboring county to Wheeling. This suggests that she was designed, or built to the specifications of these Upper Ohio men.

b) The *Wheeling Daily Intelligencer* of November 26, 1864, in reporting her maiden voyage, states, "The *Bertrand* leaves today on her *first* trip for St. Louis" (italics mine). If we can take this account literally, the "first" trip suggests that her owners planned other trips to St. Louis. This does not suggest that they originally planned to put her in the Missouri River trade and thus that they designed her for the Missouri.

c) The question of Copelin and Roe ownership of the *Bertrand* can only be settled conclusively if the Port of St. Louis enrollment records could be found. Copelin and Roe ownership would be significant to the appearance of the *Bertrand* only if they got into the act early enough to dictate her design. There is an outside possibility that, even if they chartered the *Bertrand* and didn't own her outright, they might have had some influence on the design—provided that they made their charter offer before she was completed. However, newspaper ads of the day do not suggest that they entered the picture early enough for this. Thanks to Ruth Ferris of St. Louis the following ads in the *Missouri Republican* have come to my attention. On February 13, 1865, the *Bertrand*, Yore Master, was advertised for Fort Benton, to leave on the opening of navigation. "For freight or passage apply to Capt. Jas. A. Yore. . . .Boyd & Sylvester, Agents." This same ad appeared also on Feb. 22, 23, 25, 26, 27, 28, March 1, 2, 5, 6, 11. Copelin, on the other hand, advertised only the *Deer Lodge* for Ft. Benton on Jan. 23 and Feb. 5, 1865. On February 14, Copelin, McEntire and Roe advertised for Ft. Benton, the *Deer Lodge, Benton, Yellowstone* and *Fannie Ogden.* (No mention of the *Bertrand* as late as February 14.)

Furthermore, the *Bertrand* was not sitting idle at St. Louis waiting to be purchased or chartered. In the *Missouri Republican* of Feb. 15, 1865 is an ad of the *Bertrand*, Yore Master, to leave Saturday 18 for Boonville, Brunswick, Lexington, Kansas and Leavenworth. The same paper of Feb. 19 reports that the *Bertrand* departed for Leavenworth Feb. 18. Whenever, or even if, Copelin and Roe bought or chartered the boat, the above ads do not suggest that it was early enough to dictate her design.

d) As to the physical evidence remaining on the Bertrand hull, 1) she has guards, 2) she has a model bow. Neither of these features suggest a hybrid.

As to Copelin and Roe, suppose somehow they *did* get into the act and had an influence on the design of the *Bertrand*. What was their ideal for a Ft. Benton boat? Lass, 1962, p. 43 says, "To facilitate the handling of steamboat freight in the immediate Fort Benton area, in 1865 Copelin and Roe had the light-draft steamer *Deer Lodge* constructed in Pittsburgh. This boat was kept in the Fort Union area during the navigation season of 1865 and was used only between Fort Union and Benton as a lighter for the other boats." A photo survives of the *Deer Lodge* which they "had constructed." I would call her a hybrid. Although the bow of the boat is not entirely clear in the photo, it appears to be spoonbill in shape. She has no guards. Her upper works, however, do not at all resemble the later, more typical "spoonbill mountain boats." She has stanchions and bull rails, a boiler deck cabin with hurricane roof, and no texas. Her superstructure, in fact, is typical of an Upper Ohio low-water packet.

Although this chain of reasoning is not entirely backed by iron-clad evidence, it is conclusive enough to influence my opinion until something more definite comes along to dispute it. In my opinion the *Bertrand* was an Upper Ohio River, low-water boat. Two speculations occur to me as to how she ended up on the Missouri:

1. She was built by Wheeling area people for some low-water trade in their area. The owners, before they put her into a regular local trade, and with local connections to area manufacturers, saw an opportunity to make quick profits by taking local products to the booming market at St. Louis which was supplying the gold fields. Witness the 6,000 kegs of nails on her "first" trip to St. Louis—they were probably Wheeling made, consigned to St. Louis merchants. Once in St. Louis, the owners either caught the gold fever themselves and decided to take their *Bertrand* to Fort Benton for an even bigger kill, or they received such a handsome offer to sell or charter that they couldn't pass it up.

2. The Wheeling area owners built the *Bertrand* specifically to take a fling at the Fort Benton trade themselves which, if they had an ear in St. Louis, they had reason to believe would be profitable. Not being Missouri River people, they built her low-draft in the only way they knew, and also, as a hedge, in a style that they could bring back and use in a local trade if they were not successful on the Missouri or if the trade died out there. Once in St. Louis they ran into problems because Copelin and Roe had tied up all of the available experienced Fort Benton pilots or had a lock on all the freight, or some such, so they sold or chartered to them.

In either event, she would have looked like a typical Upper Ohio low-water boat, probably with no texas. Her superstructure could very well have looked about like that of the *Deer Lodge,* built about the same time. The cabins for the *Bertrand* and the *Deer Lodge,* incidentally, were both made at Pittsburgh, at approximately the same time.

Bert Fenn

DATING OF STEAMBOAT HULLS

Students searching for means of dating the remains of early western steamers found in an archeological context are at a distinct disadvantage compared to their counterparts with interests in ocean going craft. The very earliest builders of river steamers left behind very few hull models, fewer prints and scale drawings, and very little technical literature. And by the time the photographic record had begun, the development of the western steamboat was virtually complete. However a comparison of certain features of the *Bertrand* with the published descriptions of a few early boatwrights including those by a member of the firm that installed the Bertrand engines,[8] make it possible to elaborate on a few minor changes in structural design which may eventually prove valuable in dating such craft. Some of these modifications are known to have occurred over a relatively short period of time and to have spread rapidly and widely among boatwrights of the western steamboat industry. Careful attention to these changes would appear potentially valuable in setting up criteria which might be applied to identify hull remains in time and place of manufacture.

As has been pointed out repeatedly by students of the western river steamer, the structural evolution of these boats was a slow process in which such features as length-to-breadth-to-depth ratios fluctuated considerably in various sizes and classes of vessels from the early to late 19th century (Hunter, 1949, pp. 61-120). In general, it an be asserted that the hulls were built progressively longer, wider, and shallower as the need to increase broad bearings were understood. Prior to 1830, the depth of hold of almost all river steamers measured over 8 feet, and thereafter decreased with the introduction of rectangular framing and the increased length and breadth of the vessels. However, builders continually experimented throughout the steamboat era, and substanial and widespread changes in such ratios over short periods of time are not in evidence. Thus, the size of craft

---

[8]Installed by A. J. Sweeney & Son, ironworks and manufacturer of steamboat engines in Wheeling, W. Va. The son, John M. Sweeney, was an active member of the American Society of Mechanical Engineers and a contributor of learned papers on the construction of western riverboats. He is referred to by a contemporary Wheeling historian as a "mechanic of exceptional skill." (*See* Newton, ed., 1879, pp. 236, 262; Sweeney, 1888, 1894).

and dimensional ratios are not good indicators of date or place of manufacture.

Insofar as most wooden components of supersturcture consisted of flimsy material at best, and the comparative ease with which they were almost universally removed from sunken craft by salvors, such parts cannot be expected to have survived except in the most extraordinary circumstances. Similarly, the engines and driving mechanism of most sunken steamers, while offering a much better potential for identification than either hulls or superstructure, rarely escaped the winches of the insurors' divers (King, 1863, pp. 182, 183; *Cincinnati Gazette*, Sept. 30, 1879). As early as 1838 diving bells were employed in underwater salvage operations, and men such as James B. Eads of St. Louis were contracting with insurance companies to recover engines, cargo and even entire vessels with his small fleet of "bell boats" (*Cincinnati Gazette*, Nov. 20, 1855). In some instances the underwriters stood to gain as much as 75 percent of all property they saved.[9]

A more fertile area of research should involve study of changes in the construction of the hull of western river steamers—that portion of the vessel most likely to survive the vicissitudes of time, current, conditions of soil, and the activities of salvors. Scarcely 10 years after the *Bertrand* was built, certain hull modifications, which at first glance may seem of little consequence, were incorporated into many upper-river stern wheelers. One of the more important developments, very shortly after the construction of the *Bertrand*, was the introduction of bustles coupled with a long stern rake—in contrast to the short or steep rake of the *Bertrand* and low-water boats built before her. These bustles, or bulges, in the stern resulted when depressions were made in the hull bottom to accept the throw of the forward portion of the rudder (Sweeney, 1888, p. 651, figs. 266, 268; Bates 1968, p. 19, fig. 21). The earlier practice of constructing the stern of these steamers with a short rake was popularly supposed to have increased the bearing of the hull, helped support the driving mechanism, and induced a lighter draft. But the introduction of the balance rudders which extended far under the long stern rake was found to decrease vastly the resistance of water under the hull without substantially affecting draft. In addition, the older method of setting the rudder post and pintle at a 90-degree angle from the keel line, as in the case of the *Bertrand*, was modified, and the rudder assembly was often set at an angle from the vertical so that the pintle

---

[9] *See* Eads and Nelson *vs.* The Steamboat H. D. Bacon, 1 Newberry 280 (New York 1857). For an account of the experiences of a salvor active for over 20 years in the recovery of cargo and entire vessels, see *Cincinnati Gazette*, April 11, 1868.

and upper rudder assembly tilted toward the bow (*cf.* fig. 83; Sweeney, 1888, figs. 266, 268).

Another development which occurred about 1875 that should be useful in the dating of hull remains of western stern wheelers in an archeological context was the switch from what builders referred to as bustles "built on" to those which were "built in." When the extended balance rudder associated with the long stern rake was first employed—apparently very shortly after the *Bertrand* was constructed—movement of the rudder from its neutral position to its extreme throw to either side resulted in a constantly increasing space between the upper portion of the blade projecting forward under the stern rake and the bottom of the boat. This space was considered objectionable by operators inasmuch as it had a tendency to catch drifting objects and diminish the effectiveness of rudder action. The builders then spiked blocks of wood to the bottom planking along the area of rudder travel, hung a skeleton rudder in position, and carefully shaved the blocks down along the travel of the rudder so that the space remained constant throughout the throw. This was referred to as "building a bustle on." Sometime in the mid-1870s builders in the upper Ohio area rapidly accepted a new development in which the bottoms of the frames and floor of the stern hull were modified into the required conical shapes to accept the rudder travel and the attached blocks under the stern hull were dispensed with. This change, which seems to have been diffused very rapidly among builders of stern wheelers, was referred to as "building a bustle in" (Sweeney, 1888, pp. 650-651).

There must necessarily be exceptions to the structural characteristics of western river steamers and construction periods listed below, since changes in hull design, engines, and superstructure did not develop apace among all boatwrights and yards. Although the evolution of the western steamer involved slight changes over a period of 80 years, the following major features can be identified as having been characteristic of the time frames:

1800-1820: Earliest river steamers were characterized by deep, well rounded, carvel built hulls with projecting keels and very marked sheer fore and aft. Double framed hulls housed engines, boilers, firebox, and cargo. Bowsprits and figureheads were common and the helm was located aft on main deck; some vessels retained masts and sails. First engines were of the low pressure, condensing exhaust type featuring walking beams, single vertical cylinder designed to produce maximum piston thrust on vacuum stroke. Popularity of high pressure engine initiated by Oliver Evans spread rapidly about 1815. (See House Ex. Doc. 21, 25,

Cong. 3 Sess., p. 319; Russell, 1841; Allaire and Marestier's sketches in Hunter, 1949, pp. 134, 135; and Hodge, 1840).

1821-1840:   The period of maximum change in which western river steamers achieved classic lines. Rounded hulls gave way in the middle of the period to rectangular, single framing; the keel was either reduced to a vestige or eliminated in early part of the period. Central keelsons were built within the hold; continued employment of marked sheer of as much as 3 feet fore and aft; introduction and widespread use of hog chain systems of support; stern wheels were located in a recess within hull; a trend from rounded to rectangular housings for paddle wheels on side wheelers. The superstructure was characterized as topheavy in appearance, boxlike; most vessels in late portion of period contained three decks or more including a main, boiler, and hurricane. Preference for high pressure (100 pounds per square inch or better) engines featuring single or two horizontally bedded cylinders spread throughout industry in the middle part of the period, and became standard by end of period. Paired side wheel engines were introduced around 1825; engine firebox, and boilers were moved to main deck in early portion of the period.

1841-1860:   Paddle wheels on side wheelers were generally encased in circular housings; wheels on stern wheelers moved in late years of the period from a recess to extend beyond the stern; projecting keel was eliminated; reduction (but not elimination) of sheer to slight rise of from 1 to 1 1/2 feet fore and aft; practice of constructing short rakes in stern with skegs; near universal adoption of long, horizontal cylindrical boilers; reduction in the number of decks, especially on upper-river craft to a main and boiler deck only, although on larger craft the texas deck became widespread by 1850. Early in the period the evolvement of the high pressure engine was nearly complete, characterized by closely integrated valve mechanism, crosshead guides, valve gear rods running to paddle wheel shaft.

1861-1880:   Further minor modification in hulls were adopted including long rake of bow and stern with the introduction and widespread acceptance of the bustle, *ca.* 1870. Further modification of the bustle ("built in") adopted and spread widely, *ca.* 1875; wing rudders nearly eliminated by 1870. Characteristics of the stern wheel, shallow-water steamer fully developed, including the incorporation of the wheel assembly with the hogchain trussing system and the use of multiple balance rudders.

To supplement this summary, those faced with the problem of dating the remains of river boats in an archeological context, exclusive of data that might be obtained from cargo, will do well to consult the few sources available on the construction of the western steamer. These include Hunter, 1959; Hall, 1884; Sweeney, 1888, 1894; Wallace, 1853; Tredgold, 1851; N.S. Russell, 1861; J.S. Russell, 1841; Hodge, 1840; King, 1863; Myers, 1952; and the *Wheeling Bridge Case* (1851). Inasmuch as the boatwrights and manufacturers of engines for river steamers learned their trade by experience and transmitted their knowledge primarily by word of mouth, each builder developed a few specific techniques while adhering to a body of generally accepted practices. It is obvious from the literature that the boatwrights thoroughly enjoyed experimentation and were often willing to risk a good deal of time and money on modifications. Even at the end of the era of the western river steamer, some builders were still arguing the merits of low and high pressure engines, the optimum shape of the hull below the waterline, and the ratios of length-to-breadth-to-depth.

CONDITION OF THE HULL

At the Bertrand site in the late fall of 1969, just prior to the time the well-point system was removed, allowing the water table to rise to its normal level of approximately 10 feet below ground surface, concern was expressed on the part of a number of persons intimately

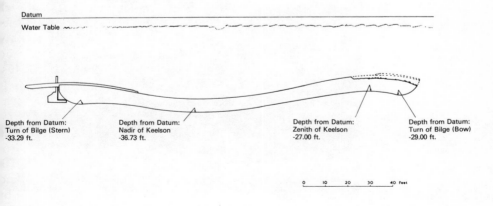

Figure 89. Conformity of *Bertrand* and its relationship to level of datum and the water table.

Figure 90. Side view (to port) of interior of hull, 59 feet to rear of stem-piece. Note futtock or "cocked hat" at bottom of photograph set at 45 degree angle. The notches cut in the side ribs (top) are set to receive deck beams and outriggers. The scarf joint of the interior supporting strake to the right of the paper tag numbered 60 has collapsed.

Figure 91. Side view (to port) of interior of hull, 105 feet to rear of stem piece. Note collapse of scarf joint of interior supporting strake, a major structural component.

associated with the project—the author included—that the boat might suffer considerable damage should attempts be made in the future to raise it by mechanical means or flotation without exercising extraordinary precautions.

Ray M. Seborg, Consultant in Wood Products for the U.S. Forest Service and an eminent authority on the cellular structure of wood, stated that the apparent extensive checking of the hull would not substantially increase if the boat were again exposed to the free oxygen atmosphere, but might suffer considerable damage if the boat were to be raised by means other than flotation, (personal communication, see also Appendix B). Furthermore, it was his and others' opinion that the supporting metal bolts, straps, and other braces holding together the major structural members of the hull were sound, despite the century and more of submergence. The fears expressed by archeologists and engineers who examined the structure were related rather to that damage which occurred to the boat as the result of its sinking in 1865, the activities of the early day salvors and recent excavation, the lightness and flexibility of the hull, and the removal of certain portions in 1969 to provide access to the cargo, notably the decking and supporting carlines or deckbeams.

In 1865, when the insurance company divers removed virtually the entire hog chain truss system along with the superstructure, the flexible hull settled and the bottom conformed to a depression (fig. 89). The strain on the major supporting strakes on the interior sides of the hull at the nadir of this depression forced the strakes and side planking apart and out of horizontal line (figs. 90, 91). In addition, this placed a considerable strain on the bolts and straps securing the ribs to the strakes and planking. Should thorough drying of these timbers occur in the future, the resulting contraction or shrinkage of the wood will almost certainly loosen the entire hull assembly and further weaken the structure amidships. Furthermore, should the hull planking on the bottom near the depression rupture or have a tendency to return to its original conformity upon drying and the release of pressure, the problem would be further compounded.

Certain other activities of the insuror's divers resulted in weakening major structural members, the inner port cylinder timber in particular. Upon excavation, it appeared that they had used a saw to cut nearly through this massive support at a point about 3 feet from the transom (fig. 92). During the time cargo was being removed from this immediate area and under the timber itself, a noticeable loosening of the entire framework of the cylinder supporting system was observed, the direct result of freeing the timber from the supporting mud, silt, and cargo. Without the latter support, only a few 1-inch metal rods running vertically from the bottom of the timbers to the

Figure 92. Activity of the early day salvors can be seen in this photograph of the inner cylinder timber, port side. Note the cut made by the saw which nearly truncated the huge timber and sliced into the bilge hatch at right-center. The remarkable aspect of this feat is the probability that it was accomplished under water, with crude diving equipment.

hull keep the loosened portion of the timbers from collapsing altogether.

Still another area of weakness and potential trouble, should attempts be made to raise the boat without precautions, is located 1⁵ feet to the rear of the stempiece. Either the result of the snag reported to have caused the sinking, or the subsequent settling over some sort of ridge, the bottom hull members at this point suffered what appears to be a sharp bend or break, causing the extreme portion of the bow to dip (fig. 89). Upon inspection, a few of the bottom planks were found to have split, although the full extent of the damage will require much closer examination of the bottom of the hull in this area. The fracture in the bow area resulted in considerable upward buckling and strain of the side strakes similar to, but in the opposite direction from, that mentioned for the side strakes amidships.

Other weaknesses include the loosening of a number of bolts holding supporting strakes to ribs and bilge keelsons to the knuckles and the broken set of forward boiler supporting beams which also serve to keep the sides from collapsing inward and straining the chines (fig. 93).

The unstable nature of the bow portion of the hull was brought to the attention of the author in July of 1969 after a series of unforeseen circumstances caused the bow portion from the point of the hull bottom break to the stempiece to rise suddenly. Prior to the day this incident occurred, the author assigned a small crew to dig a 5 by 10 foot trench immediately outside the starboard side, approximately 15 feet to the rear of the stempiece. This was undertaken in an attempt to determine and record through scale drawings the turn of the hull and to define the limits of the ice shield. The workmen, having nearly completed the digging in one day, resumed the work next morning only to find that the 10-inch pump, largest of the two in operation, suddenly malfunctioned. This pump had been evacuating nearly 70 percent of the water in the excavation, and its failure caused the water table to rise 5 feet within a matter of 30 minutes. The rising table immediately filled the test excavation with water, followed by silt. The extreme forward portion of the bow, which had been exposed and had been drying for three weeks, was quite buoyant, and the rush of water and silt under the bow lifted it suddenly, accompa-

Figure 93.   Top view of hull bottom, cargo removed, at a point directly over the boiler area. The forward boiler beams have collapsed.

nied by the creaking strain of the bottom planking, the vibrations of which could be felt throughout the boat hull. Later in the day, when the pump had been repaired and was working to reduce the water table down to its previous level, the depth of the bow below datum was again recorded with a Gurley transit, and was found to have risen 6 1/2 inches. This experience demonstrated to all concerned that certain portions of the major structural members of the hull are in a very weakened condition, and no further attempts at excavating around the periphery were made.

One more major structural weakness should be mentioned. Apparently either at the time of sinking, or when the early salvors removed the paddle wheel from its pillow blocks, much of the weight of the stern of the boat appears to have rested temporarily on the master and slave rudders on the port side. At any rate, these two were broken away from the stern posts and are no longer hinged to the hull itself.

This account is not intended to discourage a possible plan to raise the boat mechanically or by flotation should such a decision be made, but rather it is meant to encourage the employment of some system to truss or otherwise buttress the entire hull prior to any such attempt. Whatever form it takes, whether by a hog chain system similar to that originally constructed to afford rigidity, or through the use of other devices, the need to retain the contorted shape of the boat if moved as a single unit is patent.

ALTERNATIVES OF PRESERVATION

In late spring of 1970, a number of officials of the Bureau of Sport Fisheries and Wildlife, the National Park Service, and representatives of construction and salvage firms met in Minneapolis for the purpose of investigating alternative methods of preserving and exhibiting the remains of the *Bertrand*. This meeting, arranged by the National Planning Team of the Bureau of Sport Fisheries and Wildlife, was considered by all parties as a very preliminary discussion in the search for an optimum method of preserving and exhibiting the boat and the alternatives discussed[10] are summarized very generally as follows:

    1.   Retention of the hull in its present position, preserving the hull in a dry state, enclosed in a below-ground-level structure with controlled atmosphere.

---

[10]From notes compiled by Joseph Knecht, Edward Crozier, and Charles Johnston, National Planning Team, Bureau of Sport Fisheries and Wildlife. Ms on file: Office of Archeology and Historic Preservation, National Park Service, Washington D.C.

2.   Retention of the hull in its present position, building an enclosure shell around it, preserving the hull in a dry state enclosed in a structure extending above grade with controlled air atmosphere.

3.   Raising the hull intact above the existing water table, building an enclosure shell around it, preserving the hull in a dry state with controlled air atmosphere.

4.   Displaying the hull in its present position encased in a "swimming pool" enclosure, a controlled water atmosphere complete with filtering and water treatment devices. Visitor viewing from under groundwater level room adjacent to boat hull.

5.   Displaying the hull in its present position in a partially controlled, underwater atmosphere, removing all or a portion of sand around hull and the installation of underwater lighting. Visitor viewing from overhead platform.

6.   Raising the hull intact and exhibiting it dry, above water in an uncontrolled air atmosphere; the construction of a protective roof over hulk.

7.   Dewatering and re-excavating portions of the hull for removal and use in interpretive display.

A number of problems inherent in exhibiting and preserving the hulk in an underwater atmosphere were brought to the attention of those concerned, not the least of which involves the complexities of maintaining stable water temperature; the use of chemical or other agents to discourage or eliminate microbes and other organisms, and the possible corrosive action they might have on wood and metal; filtering systems to ensure water clarity; the possible adverse oxygination and decomposition of wood fiber that might result from the use of the above systems, not to speak of costs of installation and continued maintenance. Despite the dramatic impact underwater exhibition might have on the visiting public, participants in attendance at the meeting were also cognizant of the above difficulties applicable to alternatives 4 and 5 above.

---

[11]Memorandum from Ronald R. Switzer, museum specialist, National Park Service, to Joseph Knecht, architect, National Planning Team, Bureau of Sport Fisheries and Wildlife, May 15, 1970; Ms on file: Midwest Archeological Center, National Park Service, Lincoln, Nebr. Mr. Switzer's memorandum and the opinion of Dr. Seborg (Appendix B) stress the feasibility of stabilizing the wood economically through controlled, slow drying and the manner in which preservatives might be applied should the decision be made to remove the boat from the water.

Given the major options of exhibiting and at the same time preserving the hulk in a wet or dry state, the consensus of those involved who are most familiar with the conservation of the boat were in agreement on the feasibility and relative advantages of the latter, i.e., the dry preservation.[11] Such an alternative as number 6, in which the boat would be raised and presumably exhibited in an uncontrolled air atmosphere involves problems of long term wood deterioration, and number 7, of both quality of preservation and interpretive value.

As discussed above, problems inherent in the raising of the hulk either by mechanical means or by flotation which would be included in the selection of alternatives 1, 2, and 3, involve a weakened structure damaged by sinking and early salvaging activity which, even in its original condition, required a suspension system. Despite such problems, however, the flotation of long buried craft in fresh water has been accomplished where some conditions were at least similar to that in which the *Bertrand* was found. In 1966, the National Historic Sites Service of Canada successfully raised a late 18th or early 19th century British gunboat from Patterson Bay (Brown's Bay), an inlet on the north shore of the St. Lawrence River. The remains of the gunboat lay in about 6 feet of water and were nearly covered by sand. The boat was raised by an underwater archeological team by means of a large wooden cradle, constructed in such a way that the weakened remains could be suspended by canvas belts and steel cables, and floated by means of wooden tanks pumped full of styrofoam pellets (Zacharchuk and Rick, 1969, pp. 7-11).

While actual methods and details of raising or otherwise exhibiting and preserving the boat are still under study, some consideration has been given to raising the boat mechanically and retaining its distorted form by means of columns, cables, and a cradle, the former of which could be used to support a roof.[12]

---

[12]*See* "Study Report—Man, Wildlife, and the Missouri River," (n.d.), U.S. Department of the Interior, Bureau of Sport Fisheries and Wildlife, Washington D.C.

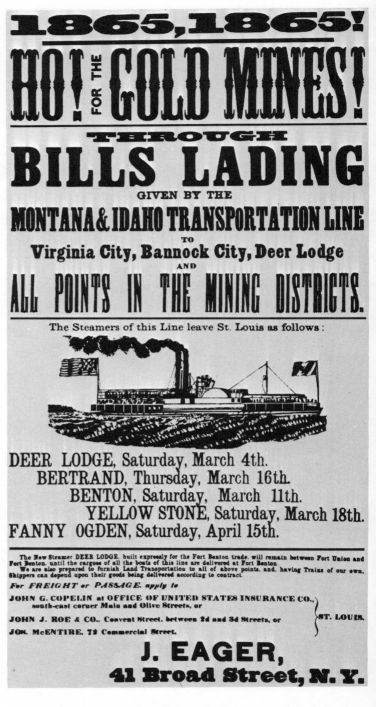

Figure 94. Handbill heralding the Bertrand's departure from St. Louis.

PART 6

THE ROLE
OF
THE BERTRAND
ON THE FRONTIER

Nearly half a century had passed from 1817 when the *Independence* arrived at St. Louis, the first steamboat on the Missouri, and the time of the Bertrand voyage. During these years, steamboating grew steadily on the upper river, spurred very early by Major Stephen H. Long's Yellowstone Expedition of 1819. In 1820, under his command, the famed *Western Engineer* ascended to the foot of the lower rapids, a feat of no little consequence for the steamer that is thought to have been one of the first stern wheelers ever built (Lass, 1962, p. 6; Chittenden, 1903, p. 570). By 1829, regular packet runs were made to Fort Leavenworth from St. Louis, but it was not until 1846 that steamboating on the upper portion of the river expanded substantially beyond the activities of the American Fur Company and a few minor rivals (Briggs, 1929, pp. 159-182; Hunter, 1949, p. 47). As early as 1833 the company's *Yellowstone* reached Fort Union, but 26 more years would pass before the first steamers reached Fort Benton in 1859—the *Chippewa* and *Key West*—just 6 years before the *Bertrand* was scheduled for the trip.

In contrast to the heavy traffic on eastern rivers and the lower Mississippi, the upper Missouri was a mere hinterland of steamboating. The voyages of the *Chippewa* and *Key West*, 3,600 miles above the mouth of the Missouri to the foothills of the Rockies of western Montana, and 3,300 feet above sea level, were the culmination of a 40-year evolutionary period of experimentation with basic structural design and maneuvering techniques to negotiate the farthest navigable reaches of the great rivers.

By the time of the *Bertrand's* construction, the classic lines and mechanics of shallow water steamers were set, combining features and structural elements derived from many sources, including

115

sea going craft, the flatboat, keelboat, and even the pirogue—the latter two of which were capable of carrying heavy cargo up the shallow rivers prior to and for a considerable period of time following the introduction of steam powered vessels. Attempts were still being made by St. Louis and Ohio river boatwrights to lessen the draft of the low-water steamers with lighter engines and boilers, and straining to the limits Federal regulations on the size and strength of boiler plate. A few minor developments in hull design were still underway, including experimentation in the design of bow shapes, rudder assemblies, and stern rakes, but the giant strides had been made.

The long, low, flat hull of the *Bertrand* and others of her day exemplifies the rule-of-thumb construction at the end of a trial-and-error period which resulted in upper river craft that drew as little as 18 inches empty and little more than 4 feet loaded. Riverboat humorists of the day spoke of floating such craft on "a heavy dew," or in Arabia, or on the suds of a recently tapped keg of beer. Even the navigation techniques were well developed by the time of the *Bertrand*, and would change very little during the remaining period of steamboat activity on the upper Missouri which, for most purposes, ended shortly after the turn of the century. In retrospect, the ingenuity of the early mechanics and boatwrights seems all the more remarkable when one considers that less than 60 years had passed from the time such classic low-water steamers were constructed in great numbers in the upper Ohio river areas, and the time of such men as Robert Fulton, Oliver Evans, and John Fitch who first experimented with steam power and the deep hulled river vessels on the East coast.

Even as the apex in the development of the mountain boats such as the *Bertrand* was reached, the demands for their use in the northwestern frontier was most urgent. In less than a decade, from 1860 to 1867, Fort Benton would experience the beginning, rise, and peak of its steamboat activity, and thereafter suffer a steady decline in river traffic in favor of the railroad (Petersen, 1955, pp. 97-120). While not all freight and passengers transported to the gold mining area in 1865 arrived in Fort Benton, a substantial percentage must have passed through. Joseph LaBarge, an experienced observer of upper river traffic and a long time riverboat captain, estimated that about 1,000 passengers and 6,000 tons of merchandise were carried into the upper Missouri in 1865, a good portion of which passed through Fort Benton.[1] Until it sank in the spring of 1865, the *Bertrand* was destined to participate in this activity and growth of the frontier at nearly the height of the gold boom.

---

[1]For a discussion of the other important alternative of transportation to Montana Territory at the time, the overland wagon train, *see* White, ed., 1966.

Prior to the discovery of gold in Montana in 1862, the upper river transportation was limited, in general, to government exploration, activities of the American Fur Company, including its transportation of Indian annuities and government supplies, and the transportation of a few settlers to the Dakota Territory in 1859 when it was opened (Lass, 1962, pp. 12-15). Immediately following the Civil War, prospectors, merchants, and adventurers of various persuasions, spurred by the flash of gold, would increase the number of steamboat arrivals at Fort Benton to 31 in 1866, 39 in 1867, 35 in 1868, and 24 in 1869. Thereafter, the decline was rapid (*ibid.*, p. 21).

When one compares the size of the ill-fated *Bertrand*, measuring 251 tons, to the capacities of other steamers operating in the upper portion of the Missouri in 1865, the loss to frontier commercial and trade interests and the intense demand for manufactured goods are brought into sharp focus.

The following "mountain" steamers reached Fort Benton, Fort Buford, and Fort Union in 1865. The list, extracted from Larpenteur's journal (Coues, 1962, pp. 423-427) has been cross-checked with the Lytle list of steamships for tonnage, construction and disposition. Steamers marked with an asterisk reached either Fort Benton or the mouth of the Marias in 1865.[2]

*Yellowstone** (Enr. No. 27519), side wheel, 378 tons, constructed at Cincinnati in 1864; first home port: St. Louis; lost in 1867 (Lytle, p. 207).

*Deer Lodge** (Enr. No. 6228), stern wheel, 493 tons, constructed at Pittsburgh in 1865, first home port: St. Louis; converted to barge in 1874 (Lytle, p. 46).

Benton (Enr. No. 2667), stern wheel, 246 tons, constructed at McKeesport, Pennsylvania, in 1864; first home port: St. Louis; lost in 1869 (Lytle, p. 19).

*Effie Deans,** stern wheel, 238 tons, constructed at Madison, Indiana, in 1863; first home port: Louisville, Kentucky; lost in 1866 (Lytle, p. 54).

*St. Johns** (Enr. No. 22644), stern wheel, 309 tons, constructed at Wheeling, West Virginia, in 1864; first home port: Wheeling, West Virginia; lost in 1875 (Lytle, p. 75).

---

[2]*See* also Anon., "Steamboat Arrivals at Fort Benton, Montana, and Vicinity," *Contributions to the Historical Society of Montana,* vol. 1, Rocky Mountain Publishing Company (Helena, 1876).

General Grant, stern wheel, 172 tons, constructed at Monongahela, Pennsylvania, in 1863; first home port: Pittsburgh; lost in 1866 (Lytle, p. 71).

Kate Kearney (Enr. No. 14075), stern wheel, 445 tons, constructed at Belle Vernon, Pennsylvania, in 1864; first home port: St. Louis; lost in 1871 (Lytle, p. 106).

Lillie Martin (Enr. No. 14979), stern wheel, 210 tons, constructed at Freedom, Pennsylvania, 1863; first home port: Pittsburgh; lost in 1867 (Lytle, p. 112).

Twilight*, side wheel, 230 tons, constructed at St. Louis in 1865; first home port: St. Louis; lost in 1865 (Lytle, p. 190).

Oronacke (sic?) (no record in Lytle).

Fanny Ogden, side wheel, 417 tons, constructed at Madison, Indiana, in 1862; first home port: St. Louis; lost in 1866 (Lytle, p. 63).

David Watts (Enr. No. 6612), stern wheel, 293 tons, constructed at Paducah, Kentucky; first home port: Paducah; lost in 1870 (Lytle, p. 46).

Hattie May, stern wheel, 230 tons, constructed at Wheeling, West Virginia, in 1864; first home port: Wheeling; lost in 1866 (Lytle, p. 82).

Cutter (Enr. No. 5295), side wheel, 92 tons, constructed in Anoka, Minnesota, in 1863; first home port: St. Paul, Minnesota; lost in 1869 (Lytle, p. 44).

Sam Gaty (no record in Lytle).

Prairie State (Enr. No. 19775), side wheel, 184 tons, constructed at Wellsville, Ohio, in 1863; first home port: St. Louis; abandoned in 1872? (Lytle, p. 156).

Converse (no record in Lytle).

Big Horn (Enr. No. 2278), stern wheel, 312 tons, constructed at New Albany, Indiana, in 1865; first home port: St. Louis; lost in 1873 (Lytle, p. 19).

A very rough estimate of the loss to the northwest frontier of foodstuffs, building supplies, etc., can be made by simply computing the measured tonnage of the *Bertrand* as a percentage of the total tonnage of all craft known to have arrived at Fort Benton in 1865. The measurement of the *Bertrand* at 251 tons compared to the total tonnage of the *Yellowstone, Deer Lodge, Effie Deans, St. Johns,* and *Twilight* would place that figure at approximately 13 percent. When one considers the fact that the *Cora II*, another heavily laden vessel headed for Fort Benton, was also lost that year, the impact of steamboat disasters in terms of loss of ready made tools, building supplies, and raw materials must have been felt by the entire frontier community. As pointed out by Petersen (1955, p. 109), despite the "desperate need" in the mining area for machinery and merchandise, the number of steamboat arrivals at Fort Benton in 1865, as compared to the two recorded in 1863 and the four in 1864, did not appreciably increase. It is difficult to arrive at a reasonable figure of dollar loss of cargo or transportation fees for the *Bertrand* short of discovering insurance records, but it should be pointed out that it was not uncommon for steamers to realize the full cost of their construction in one trip up to Fort Benton. Petersen's research has shown us that the amount of cargo varied considerably with the size of vessels, and that certain steamers must have realized, in one trip, much more than their annual cost of operation in addition to their construction: "In 1866 the average cargo of through freight to Fort Benton was estimated to be 290 tons at $12.50 per hundred pounds. Since cabin fare cost $300 that year it is not surprising that the 545-ton *Peter Balen* showed receipts of $102,690 and a net profit of $70,690, one of the most profitable trips ever recorded." (Petersen, 1955, p. 111)

In the early 19th century, the cargo capacity of riverboats (cargo weight) was approximately 50 percent of the number of measured tons (cubic capacity) of the vessel.[3] But by the 1860's, as pointed out by an eminent authority on vessel capacity of the period: "The figures of measured tonnage were customarily increased (from the early to the mid-19th century) by one-third to one-half to obtain the approximate capacity of a boat for cargo, giving an increase in capacity over the first vessels of as much as 200 percent. In effect, the facilities of steamboat transportation on the western rivers during forty years multiplied not by twelvefold but more than one hundred and twentyfold. . . ." (Hunter, 1949, p. 34)

While the entire artifact collection has not been weighed, even at the conservative estimate of an average of 10 pounds of freight per cubic foot of available space in the hull holds, the weight of the *Bertrand's* freight, exclusive of that which might have been carried on the decks, would have scaled about 210,000 pounds. That this was only a fraction of the total cargo carried on the boat seems clear given the evidence that the main deck and guards of most steamers headed for Fort Benton were usually fully loaded. In point of fact, the hold areas were generally considered less desirable for storage of

---

[3]The method of measuring tonnage on western river craft and the relationship of those figures to actual cargo capacity (by weight) is a highly complex subject. Methods changed from time to time, and were regulated by Federal law. For a concise review, see Hunter, 1949, p. 643, or Lyman, 1945, p. 223 ff.

cargo than the main deck. Since the cargo capacity of most steamers in the 1860's and 1870's was almost double that of the registered tonnage of the vessels, it would appear that the *Bertrand* might well have been capable of carrying loads of up to 400 tons. Viewed from this perspective, it is entirely possible that the insurance company which first salvaged the steamer may have recovered well over half of the cargo at the time the superstructure was removed.

The aggressive and speculative spirit which characterized the West during the steamboat era is nowhere better reflected than in the anticipated short life span of the typical upper-river steamer in the middle of the 19th century. A review of the history of those craft (listed above for which there are reliable records) operating on the upper Missouri in 1865 reveals that the average life span was slightly greater than 4 years. This figure is a somewhat better average than the 2.86 years recorded for all western steamers at about the middle of the century, and approximately the same as that estimated for all such craft in the 1860's and 1870's when rigid inspection was mandatory (Hunter, 1949, pp. 100 and 649).

Viewed from a historical perspective, the fate of the *Bertrand* serves as an important example of the hazards of river transportation during the early navigation of the upper Missouri. By the turn of the century, the Missouri River Commission of the U.S. Corps of Engineers became alarmed when the full impact of these dangers to shipping were realized. In an attempt to determine the causes of the many steamboat disasters, Capt. Hiram M. Chittenden of the Corps queried the oldest and most experienced pilots in 1897, and was able to account for the loss of 295 steamboats on the Missouri to that date (Chittenden, 1897). According to his account, the numbers and causes of wrecks were distributed as follows:

Snags	193
Ice	26
Fire	25
Rocks	11
Bridges	10
Boiler explosions	6
Sand bars	4
Storm and wind	2
Bank collisions	1
Vessel collisions	1
Overloading	1
Swamped in eddy	1
Unknown	14
Total	295

Despite evidence that only a portion of the *Bertrand* cargo or the boat itself could have been insured, reflecting a widespread practice of underwriters who refused to take full risks on any western steamer (32d Cong., 1st Sess., S. Ex. Doc. 42, p. 111), the loss to shippers and owners must be viewed in the light that the stakes of the gamble were high—so high in some cases, that a single such journey, if successful, paid for the boat with a substantial profit over and above its cost.

The Montana and Idaho Transportation Line and the individuals who owned the *Bertrand* were clearly attempting as much of a trade monopoly to and on the frontier as was possible in a time when the demands for goods were giving every indication of rocketing upward; and the men appear more than willing to have taken the risk. In the first place, it is significant that scarcely over a handful of western river steamers at St. Louis were capable of making the journey all the way to Fort Benton in 1865, and the line which owned the *Bertrand* dispatched four that year. At least one of them, the *Deer Lodge*, was constructed in Pittsburgh the year before, following Roe and Copelin's specification for use in the upper Missouri trade (Lass, 1962, p. 43). Although we cannot be certain, the specifications for the *Bertrand* may also have been drawn by the two men. The *Deer Lodge*, with a tonnage measurement somewhat larger than that of the *Bertrand*, was made with such a shallow draft that it was used as a lighter from Cow Island to Fort Benton during the entire navigation season of 1865, and there is no apparent reason why the *Bertrand* could not have been used in the same way had she not met such an unfortunate end. Secondly, the Roe and Copelin combine was in an excellent position to anticipate the growing demand for goods and transportation services. These men, with solid connections in the banking, insurance, and wholesaling businesses in St. Louis, must have carefully planned to take full advantage of the impending rush of men and supplies to Montana Territory.

While the boat owners and shippers of goods on the *Bertrand* might not have suffered heavy monetary loss, recouping a portion through insurance and probably profiting considerably from the successful runs during the season, the plight of the consumer on the frontier in 1865 was quite a different matter. The initial growth of a booming frontier community is marked by rising prices and wages, and by shortages of labor and supplies—particularly when that growth has been the result of an expectation on the part of the enterprisers that minimal returns of labor may result in maximum capital gains. Few western boom towns serve as a better example than Virginia City where a major portion of the *Bertrand* cargo was to have gone. Its newspaper editors regularly noted the rising costs of groceries, clothing, and building supplies that year, complaining in editorials of inequalities in the prices of goods and the gold dust economy which seemed to drive the prices still higher. Among the foodstuffs and household goods listed in the *Montana Post* of April 23, 1865, for example, and carried on the *Bertrand* included the following:

Flour .... 90 cents per pound
Candles .... 1 cent each
Fruits .... $25 per case of 24 cans
Raisins .... $18 per 24 lb. box
Oysters .... $30 per case of 24 cans
Sardines .... 50 cents per can
Bar Soap .... 35 cents per bar
Sugar .... 70 cents per pound

Citizens of the territory were generally aware of the reasons for the high prices, *i.e.*, the shortages of supplies brought on by the influx of prospectors in overland wagon trains and from down river, and certain individuals were in a unique position to cite other factors which contributed to the inflationary trend. Granville Stuart, one of the major consignees of the lost Bertrand merchandise and a leading merchant of the Territory, relates in his journals the loss of several wagon trains of flour and other foodstuffs from Salt Lake City during the disasterous winter of 1864-65. The trains were stranded in Beaver Canyon, a few miles from Virginia City; the oxen perished and the flour which was to have satisfied a good portion of the needs of the mining areas was lost (Phillips, ed., 1957, vol. II, p. 28). By February of 1865, the price of a 100-pound bag of flour shot up to $150, well out of reach of those who had not staked productive claims (*ibid.*, p. 27). The problem appeared so serious that residents of Virginia City feared violence, and newspaper editors suggested that some persons were hoarding the precious commodity. Stuart was a witness to what occurred:

> On April 18 word came that a large body of men armed and well organized were marching up from Nevada with the avowed determination to take possession of all the flour in town [Virginia City] and divide it among the citizens at a reasonable and fair price. This information was soon verified by the appearance of five hundred men marching in file, all armed with revolvers and rifles. . .there was no doubt of their intentions. Within five minutes after their arrival they commenced at the foot of Wallace street and searched every store and place where flour could be concealed. About one hundred twenty-five sacks were found and safely stored away in Leviathan Hall. The search was orderly but very thorough and disclosed sundry lots of flour concealed under coats, in boxes and barrels and under hay stacks. (*ibid.*, pp. 27-28)

Following seizure, the armed men set out to enforce a rule that merchants were to sell all available flour at no more than $27 to $30 per hundred pounds, and that it be rationed, 12 pounds to a single man, double for those who were married, and more if there were children in the family (*ibid.*, p. 28).

It should be of more than passing interest to the economist or historian of the frontier that, whatever else might have been in the holds of the *Bertrand*, she was carrying goods that would have substantially alleviated such food shortages. In reviewing the territorial newspapers of the period, nearly every issue contained lists of changing prices of goods which were a part of the *Bertrand's* cargo. In addition to the commodities in short supply mentioned above, Stuart listed potatoes, bacon, tea, butter, beans and hominy.

Despite the shortages of staple foods such as flour, sugar, and potatoes—and the deprivation this must have meant for some—it appears that certain segments of the frontier society could afford to set rather substantial tables. The array of condiments that was found as a part of the Bertrand cargo reflects the need to disguise the blandness of the fare, as well as the flavors of foods difficult to preserve at such a time and place. Included in the cargo were pepper and other hot sauces, whole and ground pepper, a variety of spices, hot mustard, horseradish, catsup, club and other pungent sauces, most of which were canned or bottled by eastern or St. Louis firms. Nevertheless, other products, such as French olive oil, brandied peaches and cherries, domestic and foreign wines and champagnes, oysters, imported sardines, jellies and a variety of nuts and pie fruits attest to some sophisticated tastes for occupants of the Montana mining towns, most of which at that time were only three years old. And while the majority of dry goods and clothing recovered in the holds were sturdy weaves of wool, miners' boots, shirts and trousers, included also were a number of cases of stylish men's suits and coats and fancy shawls for women. At least the outward appearances of civilization were not long coming.

Just as the variety of foodstuffs aboard the *Bertrand* was extensive, so too were the consignments of tools and other hardware, including some metal stock. A cursory examination of the contents reveal that this consisted mainly of tools and hardware that would have been difficult if not impossible to manufacture or finish on the frontier and, as might be expected, to have been made for wood and leather working. A wide variety of nails, screws, hand cutting tools, white lead for paint, and tar paper reflect the needs of the new mining towns of Virginia City, Hell Gate, and Deer Lodge. In addition to the needs of miners for woodworking in limited shaft mining and for sluices, one of the initial efforts made by prospectors, regardless of means, was to move out of tents, caves, and other quite temporary shelters into wooden structures prior to cold weather (White, 1966, pp. 221-223). A few highly specialized tools such as pipe and rod threading equipment, other metal working devices and quite an array of finished hardware such as locks, oil lamp assemblies, cartridges, bullet and candle molds, and fulminate of mercury fuses were on board and were clearly in demand.

Judging from the total contents of the *Bertrand*, mining was not the only economic base of the territory in the mid 1860s. Such devices as large butter churns, cow bells, scythes, potato and hay forks were present in considerable numbers. Perhaps most remarkable were the large number of plows and hand cultivators that were removed from the holds. Several of the Blunden Koenig plows, capable of cutting 18-inch furrows and meant to be harnessed to several braces of oxen or horses, attest to concerted activity on the part of some either to supplement mining, or make their living exclusively by agriculture in the midst of gold fever. More than two dozen plow blades of various sizes and many more plow and cultivator frames were recovered.

Unfortunately, an examination of the few passengers known to have been on the *Bertrand* is not particularly enlightening in terms of history or the population make-up of the frontier. A complete list of passengers has not been found, and what little evidence that can be brought to bear on the problem, indicates that there were no more than 20 on board (*Sunday Journal and Star*, April 12, 1936). The persons known to have been on the boat appear to comprise a rather heterogeneous group that one might expect on any trip to the mountains. The *Bertrand* was essentially a packet, and was quite obviously intended to carry a maximum amount of freight. Those who are known by name include a W. Burroughs (an Iowa attorney) and his daughter and grandchildren, a Mrs. Atchison and children, the Campbell sisters, daughters of J.B. Campbell who had settled earlier near Gallatin, a man by the name of Albert Rowe, Mr. and Mrs. H. E. Bixby and servant, and several other unidentified women (*Davenport Gazette*, April 13, 1865; Herndon House Register, April 2, 1865; Moss, ed., 1963, p. 163).

It is possible that one of the more interesting passengers, possibly the servant mentioned as having put up at the Herndon House in Omaha the day following the sinking, may have been a Chinese girl. During the excavation, a small lacquered box was found in a larger, broken case of personel possessions which could not be further identified, and on which appeared two Chinese characters in brushed gold. Transliterated, the characters refer to a girl's name, Yi-

Shing.[4] The box contained fragments of clothing and a few water-melon and other unidentified seeds. Chinese house servants, as well as considerable numbers of laundresses and laborers had already moved into the mining towns and, in such places as Last Chance (later Helena), Chinese enclaves evolved into small towns within larger communities.

Whatever else may have been the fate of the passengers, the sinking probably meant little more than a loss of a few personal possessions and an inconvenient delay. The Campbell sisters and several other women and children simply waited at DeSoto and boarded the General Grant, a steamer that followed the route of the Bertrand several days. Similar plans were no doubt made by those passengers who stayed at the Herndon House, the Omaha hotel which catered to river travellers of the day.

That most intriguing question of who recovered the vast treasure of mercury may never be certainly known. Short of locating historical evidence involving insurance or salvage, perhaps the most reasonable tentative conclusion would be that the underwriters recovered nearly all of it at the same time a few days after the sinking that their workmen were reported to have removed superstructure and some cargo. Although there is no direct evidence to support this position, a number of observations bear upon the question.

The McNeely party search for the Bertrand in 1896 cannot be altogether eliminated as a possibility, but in view of the publicity given their attempt at locating the boat (Omaha Weekly Bee, July 22, 1896) and the failure of local newspapers to follow up on such activity which must have excited the entire local populace, they would appear to have failed. It is of more than passing interest that the McNeely account in the Bee article contains certain inconsistencies and inaccuracies, despite the valid information it contained about the approximate location of the boat. When one compares such information in the Bee article with what is now known concerning the boat and its cargo, it becomes clear that McNeely, said to be a brother of one of the divers who worked for the insurance company, was misinformed.

According to the McNeely account, the Bertrand was the largest steamer that ever attempted the ascent of the river, the cargo included considerable amounts of whiskey in casks, the mercury was shipped in lead containers, and only a small portion of cargo was removed by the insurance company a few days after the sinking. However, historical and archeological evidence points to quite a dif-

---

[4]The characters were identified by Dr. Dah-Yinn Lee of Iowa State University, and Dr. Motoko Lee, a linguist at Duke University.

ferent picture. The *Bertrand* is known to have been only of average size and displacement of steamers plying the upper Missouri at the time. Only two cases of "mixed" spirits known as "Whiskey Cock-tail" were found in the holds. Furthermore, in view of the fact that the insurors were able to recover entire engines and most of the superstructure, it is quite likely that at least a third of the total cargo, *i.e.*, that on the main deck, would have been recovered as well.

    Other observations might be added in support of the contention that the insuror's divers rather than the McNeely party successfully recovered most of the mercury. At the time the nine remaining containers were found in 1969, it was noted that only four of the carboys lay directly on the hold floor. With the exception of the one found in the backdirt (removed inadvertently with the crane bucket) the others rested in random positions in a matrix of silt from 8 inches to a foot above the floor. It is quite unlikely that even severe water movement and flooding could have raised them to such a position in view of the tremendous mass of the mercury and its small containers, well over 200 pounds per cubic foot. Movement by human agency is indicated.

    At the time the McNeely search was underway in 1896, the boat was already in much the same position under about the same amount of silt and depth of water table as it was when found in 1968. Powerful pumps and other equipment that would have been required to lower the water table to the levels and over the area achieved by the Omaha salvors were unavailable in 1896. On the other hand, diving equipment in 1865 prior to the time the *Bertrand* was completely silted over was well enough developed that entire engines could be recovered under several feet of water. The removal under water of a small amount of decking in the bow to provide access to the mercury would have been quite possible, since Captain Yore must have known its precise location. Certainly attempts by the divers must have been made in view of its value. That they would have overlooked and unsuccessfully grappled for a few containers which remained for over 100 years surrounded by silt does not seem unreasonable.

    In retrospect, the question of who recovered the mercury is of little importance. Of particular and lasting significance is the impact the *Bertrand* and its interpretation at the DeSoto National Wildlife Refuge will have on future generations of Americans. The recovery of sunken vessels, the time capsules of the archeologist, has a way of mentally thrusting us back, and forcing us to grapple with that most persistent element of history—the urge to know in considerable detail what motivated men of another day. The *Bertrand* went down in exciting times, a week before the end of the Civil War, 14 days before Lincoln was shot, and at the height of the gold discoveries in

Montana. The boat and its cargo serve to bring us a little better understanding of those times, and of men who were willing to risk their lives and investments in the opening of the frontier.

The steamboat in the history of America assumes a romantic if not nostalgic role, sometimes to the point of detracting from the economic nature of its use on the rivers of our country. Thousands of steamboats were lost in the 80-year history of their use, over 400 on the Missouri River alone. The *Bertrand*, as a unique historic site, will serve as a constant reminder that the opening of the Western rivers to navigation was not accomplished without losses and temporary setbacks. One can only wonder what must have been on the mind of Captain Yore when he struck the snag and knew the *Bertrand* was lost. Perhaps his feelings are best expressed by Stanley Vestal in his book, *The Missouri*, when he wrote that "the trouble with going up the Missouri River in a boat is that you have to take the boat along."

Figure 95. A caster set found in the hold of the *Bertrand*. Such revolving condiment trays and cruets graced the dinner tables of only the more elegant mid-19th century homes. (Photo courtesy of American Telephone & Telegraph Co., Long Lines Department.)

APPENDIX A

Preservation of Bertrand Artifacts: General Procedures

—Ronald R. Switzer[1]

      The preservation of the cargo of the *Bertrand*, while a rewarding and challenging experience, has been, at times to say the least, exasperating. Few if any organizations have been charged with the responsibility of preserving an American historical and archeological treasure of such magnitude, and the demanding problems that have arisen during the course of this activity will continue. A number of specific problems contribute to the difficulty of the preservation and conservation of Bertrand artifacts, not the least of which is the sheer volume and the broad spectrum of classes of material. Unfortunately, in the early stages of the salvors' excavation, no one could have known what lay in the holds. Faced with the rights of the salvors to remove the material expeditiously, yet under supervision of National Park Service archeologists exercising professional controls, optimum conditions of preservation were not possible until adequate laboratory facilities could be installed at the refuge. Also, in the absence of qualified conservators during the very first stages of cargo removal, the safety and integrity of certain material could not be insured.

---

[1]Mr. Switzer, Superintendent of Mesa Verde National Park, was a museum specialist with the Midwest Archeological Center, National Park Service, and directed the Bertrand Laboratory at DeSoto Bend National Wildlife Refuge, and the laboratory at the Midwest Archeological Center.

The purpose of this appendix is to present a broad outline of artifact treatment. Obviously a detailed resume of specific procedures must wait for future years, when specific problems have been solved.

Major work on the cargo began in October of 1968. Artifacts removed from the steamship's hold were transported to the headquarters area at DeSoto National Wildlife Refuge where they were washed, sealed in polyethylene and stored in a vacant garage bay through the winter. Relative humidity in this temporary storage area was controlled, within reasonable limits, with the use of moist burlap bags. In the spring of 1969, when the temperature began to rise, two window-mounted air conditioners were installed at the mouth of the garage bay. Textiles were removed to the Midwest Archeological Center in Lincoln, where they were kept under refrigeration prior to cleaning.

In June, 1969, when work resumed at the excavation site, enormous amounts of cargo began to fill the maintenance yard at the Refuge. In order to keep the cargo wet, Refuge personnel immersed large quantities of artifacts in water-filled canvas tanks ranging in size from 1,000 to 10,000 gallons. By July, warm summer temperatures promoted the growth of fungi in the tanks. At the suggestion of Ray M. Seborg, a consultant from the Forest Products Research Laboratory. Thymol was added to the tanks at the rate of 5 gallons per 1,000 gallons of water to kill the various fungi. Deck planks from the *Bertrand*, which had been stored with the cargo, were removed from the tanks and stacked to dry in the maintenance yard.

Removal of cargo from the holds was completed in September, and, by October 7, all but two of the canvas tanks had been emptied and the artifacts removed to storage. Temporary shelves were constructed inside a six-bay truck garage at Refuge headquarters, and the walls of three bays were insulated with styrofoam sheets, 4 inches thick. Window air conditioners installed in each of the three bays and several small space heaters provided temperature control through the fall and winter.

At the end of October, in a makeshift laboratory in the Refuge office complex, experimental studies were begun to determine the most suitable preservation methods for the cargo. Operating with limited funds, provided by the Bureau of Sport Fisheries and Wildlife and the National Park Service, preservation methods selected were based on a number of factors, including cost, existing facilities, time, the availability of personnel, chemicals and apparatus, and reversability. Shortly thereafter, with increased availability of funds, a new artifact conservation laboratory was constructed at the refuge.

THE LABORATORY

Most, but not all, of the major preservation techniques were established by the end of June, 1970. However, experimentation to improve those methods and to deal with new problems which arose from time to time represented an ongoing activity which will never fully terminate. In October, 1970, the Bertrand Laboratory staff moved its chemicals and apparatus to the newly completed facility on the Refuge, and, with the help of Refuge personnel, moved the cargo into the permanent storage area in the new building. Atmospheric conditions in the storage area of the laboratory complex are maintained at 55°F with a relative humidity of 50 percent.

The facility was divided into functional work areas to ease congestion in dealing with the cargo. The large general laboratory was equipped with Kemresin sinks and counters mounted on steel cabinets, a safety shower, fire extinguishers, blackboard and bulletin board, flexible shaft machines, two industrial airbrasive units with glove box and dust collector, and a 500-gallon, galvanized steel holding tank. Cataloguing this vast collection was also performed in the general laboratory where the curator kept a photographic record using a Polaroid MP-3 positive-negative camera. Selected artifacts were photographed before, during and after processing with .35mm color film to supplement the record of laboratory activities. In addition, the Bertrand Conservation Laboratory was equipped for microscopic studies and micro-photography.

A second smaller laboratory was equipped with a sink, counters, cabinets, hot plates, a large mechanical convection oven, several ultra-sonic cleaning units, and apparatus for electrolytic reduction. The laboratory was equipped with blowers to evacuate the atmosphere once every nine minutes.

A third laboratory was equipped for wet chemistry and contains sinks, counters, cupboards, a large fume hood, bunsen burner, and two types of vacuum apparatus. The atmosphere in this room can be evacuated once every 12 minutes, or faster, when the fume hood is in operation.

The fourth and final section of the laboratory complex contains a chemical storage room with modular steel shelving. Light fixtures and blowers in this room are sealed and gasketed, and the concrete floor is depressed 4 inches. The chemical storage room contains a blower and duct work to evacuate the atmosphere every 9 minutes, and a water source and floor drain to flush away spilled chemicals.

The storage area of the building contains a large, shallow,

stainless steel sink, air compressors, grit blasting equipment and a bulb-lit, asbestos insulated drying oven. Floors in the cargo storage area and in all laboratories contain floor drains. In the opposite end of the building are located the crew room, lavatories, clerical supply storage room, physical equipment room, and a small artifact viewing room.

To reduce the danger of explosion and fire, diethyl ether and other dangerous chemicals are stored in a ventilated steel shed located 40 feet north of the main building. A shaded stall was constructed adjacent to the steel shed which was used during the summer months for grit blasting heavy metal objects.

PRESERVATION TECHNIQUES

The preservation techniques employed in the Bertrand Laboratory are, of necessity, quite varied inasmuch as we are treating many artifacts with unique qualities. Although, for the most part, we are preserving basic kinds of substances, there were some materials and specific artifacts that most conservators have never had to treat. Canned and bottled fruits, preserves, vegetables, shell fish, meats, sauces, honey and molasses, bitters, liquors, wines, champagne, ales, inks and tonics certainly presented unique problems. Others involved butter, soap, salt meat, matches, black powder, candles, tarpaper, white lead, and wagon grease. In addition, many items were composed of more than one material. Multi-component artifacts, in most cases, had to be disassembled and each material treated separately before they were reconstructed and catalogued.

An annotated outline of preservation techniques for major classes of materials is presented in the following pages. Wherever one method has proved more effective than others, appropriate commentary is provided.

TEXTILES

Nearly 1,600 cubic feet of textiles were recovered from the *Bertrand*, most of which are bolt and ready-made goods of wool or silk; some cotton textiles survived as well. Other items classified as textiles include several varieties of men's hats and at least one type of rubberized slicker.

So excellent was the condition of the majority of textiles that no special treatments had to be developed for purposes of cleansing and preservation. Each bundle was sampled to record the nature of the fibers, direction of spin of the fibers, type of weave, the presence of stitches, binding, selvages and applied decoration, fastness of the dyes, and the nature and amount of foreign matter present. With the exception of the dye tests, most of this information was obtained with the aid of a binocular microscope. Standard dye fastness tests using detergent, ammonia, acetic acid, and water were run on each fabric before cleaning. All data were recorded on forms similar to those used by the Textile Museum in Washington D.C.

All textiles were cleaned using deionized water and non-ionizing detergents. Fabrics were cleaned between Lumite screens in specially constructed fiberglass tanks and were dried on large Lumite screen drying racks. In many instances, commercial fabric softeners proved useful in improving the texture and appearance of the textiles, and greatly increased rinsability.

After washing and drying, the textiles were stored flat, in specially constructed boxes. Individual items are wrapped in or separated by non-acid tissue paper. Each storage box contains a dated vial of Thymol or paradichlorobenzine.

WOOD

Many artifacts are composed, at least in part, of wood. Wood artifacts, and wood parts of multicomponent artifacts have been treated with a variety of chemicals, but the most successful method involved the use of polyethylene glycol.

All but two wood preservation techniques required that the specimens be stabilized by weight in pure ethyl alcohol. The artifacts to be stabilized were first washed under running water with soft nylon brushes. Specimens stabilized in alcohol were placed in dated vats and weighed every two days until there was no appreciable change. The final recorded weight on the vat tag served as a base from which preservation absorbtion was calculated.

Some stabilized wood specimens were treated with Gelva V-7 (a nitrocellulose), butyl acetate, propyl acetate, and certain resins. The use of vacuum apparatus with these materials often improved impregnation of the artifacts. Occasionally, it was helpful to dehydrate an artifact fully before impregnation. This was accomplished by placing the specimens in successive baths of alcohol, acetone, and diethyl ether *en vacuo*. For our purposes, the most successful treatment of wood has resulted from the use of polyethylene glycol (PEG) 4000 and 6000 in an ethyl alcohol medium. Stabilized artifacts of wood were placed in PEG for various lengths of time, depending on their size and condition. Upon removal from the PEG, specimens showed a 25 percent increase in weight over that last recorded on the alcohol vat tag.

Two other techniques have been used on small wood artifacts with varying degrees of success. Neither of these techniques required that the artifacts be stabilized by weight nor fully dehydrated. Both depended on the process of osmosis for their success.

In the first technique, waterlogged artifacts were immersed in polymethacrylate or polyvinyl acetate at room temperature until impregnation was complete. The second method involved immersing the specimens in a potash-alum-glycerine-water solution maintained at near boiling until it had fully penetrated the fibers. Usually, when these techniques had been employed, the artifacts were given several light coats of Damar resin, thinned Agateen lacquer, or commercial matte spray fixative, sometimes followed by a coat of turpentine and linseed oil mixed in equal amounts.

Some wood artifacts have been left to dry under controlled conditions and none of these have suffered appreciably. Our records indicate these artifacts have shown little distortion, dimensional change, cellular collapse, splitting or checking, and in most cases there was less than 10 percent shrinkage. Controlled drying of additional specimens may have some merit as an inexpensive technique for broken and nonrestorable materials.

FERROUS METALS

Iron, tinned iron, and steel comprise the next largest class of basic materials recovered from the Bertrand. It should be noted that in no case have artifacts composed of these materials survived without damage from oxidation and corrosion. Usually a combination of preservation techniques were employed to treat iron and steel artifacts, owing to excessive deterioration. However, the basic procedures included the initial use of mechanical cleaning aids such as dental picks, wire wheels and brushes, flexible shaft machines with various attachments, industrial airbrasive units, and grit blasters. Materials and apparatus used in conjunction with mechanical cleaning aids included ultra-sonic apparatus, electrolytic reduction tanks, electrolytes for electrochemical reduction, acids, and commercial rust removers composed mainly of acids.

The larger artifacts such as plows, and the mud and steam drums from the Bertrand engine compartment, could not be immersed for lack of tanks of adequate size. These items, many of which were badly corroded, were grit blasted and coated with commercial rust removers before they were lacquered for storage.

Smaller specimens were cleaned mechanically, usually with the help of an industrial airbrasive unit set at between 45 and 80 psi, emitting 50-micron silicon carbide grit or glass beads. After the heavy dirt, corrosion, and oxidation had been removed, they were placed in one of three tanks for further treatment. Those artifacts which were in relatively good condition were placed in an ultra-sonic transducer tank and finished in Fremont 254 rust remover, composed mainly of sodium hydroxide. Other items were cleaned in one of our electrolytic tanks, or were placed directly into Fremont 254 or CRC rust remover. Items in Fremont 254 or CRC were heated to near the boiling point and the temperature of the solution was maintained throughout the process.

Each artifact treated thus had to be removed from solution from time to time and brushed under running water to remove the black sludge which accumulated on the surface.

All artifacts of iron and steel which had been processed by electrolysis or in rust removers were given alternate hot and cold water baths to flush the pores before drying in acetone. Once dry, artifacts were coated with rust inhibitors and/or sprayed with Agateen lacquer or a matte spray fixative. The best results on iron and steel artifacts were produced with Fremont 254 rust remover and mechanical descaling aids.

NON-FERROUS METALS

Non-ferrous metal artifacts from the *Bertrand* are composed mostly of brass, copper and lead, or alloys of the former such as britanium or pewter. Several bronze bearing cushions from the boat itself have also been observed in the collection.

Copper and Brass

Calcium deposits and heavy incrustations of alteration products such as cuprite, malachite and azurite were reduced in thickness using hardwood picks and glass beads at 65 psi in an industrial airbrasive unit.

Experiments have been conducted on copper and brass artifacts using a number of chemicals, including Rochell Salt and sulphuric acid, nitric acid, sodium hexametaphosphate, sodium sesquicarbonate, citric acid, and sulphuric acid in solutions of 5 to 10 percent. The best results were obtained with sodium hexametaphosphate and sodium sesquicarbonate in 5 percent solutions at room temperature. The major disadvantage of both products was the slow reaction time, but many small items could be cleaned simultaneously. Citric acid in 5 percent solutions has also produced good results. Brass or copper treated by any of these techniques were burnished with commercial metal polishes or with whiting and ammonia, precipitated chalk, or pulverized rottenstone and ammonia. Lacquer, spray matte fixative, and micro-crystaline waxes were the only fully satisfactory coatings used on brass and copper in the Bertrand Laboratory.

Other techniques have been used in the treatment of copper and brass, but the results are not wholly satisfactory, and the necessary materials are expensive. Two of the methods involved reduction with zinc and caustic soda, and electrolysis in caustic soda. The former was relatively effective, but the cost of an adequate amount of 20-mesh granulated zinc metal was prohibitive.

Because certain brass and copper artifacts were badly bent, annealing and shaping have been performed on some items, enabling better cleaning. Occasionally artifacts were shaped for cosmetic purposes to enhance the overall visual quality.

Lead and Pewter
Small numbers of lead and pewter artifacts have been processed, but none have suffered extensive damage from oxidation and corrosion. Most are in a good state of repair. For the most part, objects of lead and pewter have been treated in hydrochloric acid followed by ammonium acetate. This technique, coupled with mechanical cleaning, polishing and sealing with microcrystaline wax are the only methods used on these items at the present time.

Tin
Cans represented the major items composed at least in part of tin. The cans, of course, are tinned iron, and are not composed solely of tin. Ultra-sonic cleaning, electrolysis, and the acid treatment described for lead and pewter have produced good results. Electrolytic reduction seemed to work about as well as any method devised in the laboratory, but the volume of cans in the cargo made its use questionable. Acids were occasionally used to reduce difficult spots of iron rust.

Silver
Both sterling and plate have been observed in the cargo. Reduction with aluminum metal and sodium hydroxide, and with aluminium metal and sodium carbonate, followed by polishing with commercial silver cream were the only methods used. Mixtures of sodium carbonate, and cream of tartar and ammonia did not produce satisfactory results.

Processed silver artifacts were wrapped in acid free tissue and stored in tightly closed containers. Microcrystaline wax was the only post cleaning substance used on silver items.

Britannia

Inasmuch as the small amount of flatware made of this alloy was in excellent condition, nothing was done except minor polishing. Some pieces were bent, but straightening presented no major problems.

BOTTLES AND GLASS

Hundreds of bottles of perishables were recovered from the *Bertrand's* holds, and at least 30 different shapes and sizes are represented. In addition, the collections include a large number of glass chimneys, oil fonts and bases for lamps, and no small number of castor sets, candy dishes, salt cellars, mirrors, and glass for picture frames.

Most of the glass artifacts were in good condition, although some irridescence and deterioration has been observed. The major problems which developed with respect to the bottled perishables involved the contents of the bottles, the corks, seals and labels associated with the containers.

Bottles without contents, corks, seals and labels, and most other glass items were washed in Super Edisonite, biodegradeable cleanser for laboratory glassware with a Ph of 8. After cleaning, the artifacts were rinsed and dried in successive baths of alcohol and acetone. Later, after cataloguing, they were wrapped in soft tissue and placed in sealed, compartmented boxes built especially for glass storage. The boxes tended to create an excellent stable micro-environment.

Bottles exhibiting good corks and lead seals were treated in much the same manner, but the integrity of the cork/seal unit was maintained throughout cleansing. The seals were cleaned mechanically, with glass beads in an airbrasive unit at 65 psi and/or burnished with a soft steel bristled jeweler's scratch brush. Finally, the tops of the bottles, including the lead seals, were coated with a specially formulated resin to make the bottles airtight.

Bottles bearing paper labels were handled with great care. The glass was cleaned to the periphery of the label, and the label itself brushed lightly with a soft jeweler's brush to remove excess dirt. Most labels and label fragments did not adhere tightly to the glass; therefore, they were given a thin coat of water soluble polyvinyl acetate to consolidate the fragments and to prevent them from peeling away from the glass. Owing to the nature and condition of the paper, little could be done to remove stains from the labels.

Bottles with deteriorated corks were washed, but the corks were removed and a preservative solution was added to their contents. Preservative solutions used included formalin, ethyl alcohol, and a commercial fungicide; occasionally, combinations of these were tried. Finally, these bottles were given new corks which were sealed to the bottle glass with epoxy.

IRONSTONE AND PORCELAIN

Several barrels of ironstone dinnerware and miscellaneous pieces of porcelain have been cleaned and preserved in the Bertrand Conservation Laboratory. With the exception of breakage, most of these artifacts were in good condition and needed nothing but washing, drying and storing in a stable atmosphere.

A few pieces exhibiting iron stains were placed in dilute solutions of hydrogen peroxide, and experiments have been conducted using acids, and Versene Fe-3 with good results.

LEATHER

More than 3,000 leather boots and shoes and an undetermined quantity of book covers, wallets, whips, and harness constitute the bulk of the leather items recovered from the *Bertrand*. For the most part, the leather is in good condition, but such materials as stitching disintegrated long ago.

Leather artifacts were washed under fresh running water with medium-stiff bristle brushes to remove caked mud and dirt. After washing, these specimens were placed in a solution three times their volume of pure ethyl alcohol until their weight stabilized. When stabilization was complete, the leather was immersed in vats of sulfonated cod oil, emulsified 1:5 in water. The artifacts remained in this leather dressing until their weight again stabilized, at which time they were removed from the vats and wiped dry. Some items were then placed in Tanoyl 1230-B (a fat liquor) mixed 1:1 with water until they were super-saturated with the solution. Other leather artifacts were brushed with several applications of Tanoyl solution. Following treatment in Tanoyl, the excess solution was blotted with clean, lint free cotton rags and the artifacts were left to air dry for several days, and blotted again. Wallets, book covers, and harness, which have at least one finished side, were treated with carnauba wax and polished with a soft cloth. Excellent results have been obtained with the alcohol, sulfonated cod oil, and Tanoyl treatment. The leather is flexible and exhibits a lasting luster and resilience.

Hob nails and scuff plates on the bottoms of boots were cleaned with dolomite or 27 micron aluminum oxide using the airbrasive units at 80 psi equipped with large orifice nozzles. Subsequent to this operation, the metal was carefully burnished and coated with Agateen laquer.

Figure 96.   Fragments of Hostetter's almanacs following alternate freezing and drying processes in the laboratory. (Photo courtesy of the American Telephone & Telegraph Co., Long Lines Department.)

PAPER AND DECALCOMANIA

Very few artifacts of paper survived after 105 years underwater. Several *Hostetter's Almanacs* (fig. 96), some bottle labels, tax stamps and a few small matchbox labels have withstood the tests of time and water. Also surviving are paper and decal backed glass plates which composed the doors to pendulum boxes of six large clocks.

Inasmuch as we were not equipped to treat paper at the time, several avenues were explored. Several of the surviving almanacs were sent to the Smithsonian Institution where they were freeze-dried. Later the pages were separated and repair and cosmetic treatment was given.   Others were treated successfully in the Bertrand Laboratory by alternately freezing and drying, and separating the pages between operations.

Labels and tax stamps were carefully bathed in distilled water, blotted, and allowed to dry slowly under weighted pieces of glass. A small number of labels have been treated using the sodium hypochlorite method described in Plenderleith's *Conservation of Antiques and Works of Art*, but the results have not been promising.

Decals on the pendulum box panels adhered well, but scenes printed on paper began to peel away from their glass backing. In both cases the glass was cleaned as carefully as possible, and some attention was given to removing mud from the backs of the decals and paper. Water soluble polyvinyl acetate was brushed onto the backs of the paper scenes which helped to retain the integrity of the material and to keep it from separating from the glass. The decals were treated with PVA only if they had begun to show signs of deterioration or separation.

MISCELLANEOUS

The term miscellaneous encompasses a great variety of Bertrand artifacts. Among the more important items were canned goods, wagon grease, butter, white lead, sawdust or tow used as packing in wooden shipping boxes, black powder, salt meat and candles.

The contents of most tin cans have been or will be destroyed, as the danger of tetanus and botulism is extreme. The butter and salt meat have already been disposed of for the same reasons. Genus and species determinations of the animals represented in the salt meat sample have been made.

The wagon grease acted as a preservative for its tin containers: therefore, very little has been done to this material. The Los Alamos Scientific Laboratories at Los Alamos, N.M. is conducting experiments to attempt to determine the provenience of the oil field from which this petroleum product was obtained.

Black powder presented no problems of preservation. The potassium nitrate and sulphur components of the powder no longer exist, and all that remains of the original powder is charcoal dust. This was dried and stored in polyethylene jars. Sawdust packing material was dried in a like manner and stored in polyethylene bags.

White lead, presumably shipped for use in making house paint, has become rock hard, and nothing was done to preserve it other than drying and storing in suitable containers. The lead was not put back in its original kegs after they were processed and reconstructed.

Tallow candles are the final item to be considered in this section. Most were in good condition and retained their cotton wicks. They required little processing except soaking in dilute hydrochloric acid, brushing under running water and drying in acetone.

Only a general statement regarding artifact preservation has been possible in this appendix. However, as research continues on preservation methods at the Bertrand Conservation Laboratory, the information accumulated will be compiled as a manual for use by conservators.

APPENDIX B

Inspection
of the Bertrand:
A Preliminary Report[1]

—Ray M. Seborg

I inspected the wood of the steamboat *Bertrand,* and some of the wooden artifacts that had been removed from the boat on Sept. 16 and 17, 1969. I was accompanied by Terry Highley, pathologist, U.S. Forest Products Laboratory, Madison, Wis. The history of the steamboat, and the work that was being carried on at the excavation were explained to me by Jerome E. Petsche, archeologist on the site, Wilfred D. Logan, Chief of the Midwest Archeological Center, and Carl Semczak, preservator, all of the National Park Service, and Wayne Chord, Assistant Manager of the DeSoto National Wildlife Refuge.

Excavation of the interior of the steamboat was sufficiently complete to reveal most of the wood structure. The deck had been removed to allow removal of the cargo, and inspection of the planking and timbers could readily be made. Cargo that had been removed was carefully wrapped to prevent drying, and was stored in a cooled atmosphere or under water. Most of the cargo that had been removed consisted of products other than wood. The wood artifacts that I noted were packaging crates, kegs, buckets, and tool handles. Some kegs, staves from buckets, boards from crates, and shovel handles had been

---

[1]Submitted to the Midwest Archeological Center by Ray M. Seborg, Consultant in Wood Products, Forest Products Laboratory, U.S. Forest Service. Mr. Seborg's preliminary investigation was undertaken prior to complete excavation of the *Bertrand* to examine the characteristics of boat and cargo wood, and to advise on means of preservation.

142

treated with polyethylene glycol-4000. The treatment, as explained by Mr. Carl Semczak, was accomplished by soaking the wet wood in alcohol and then immersing the wood in a 50 percent solution of alcohol-polyethylene glycol-4000 maintained at 65° C for various periods of time, depending on thickness of material, followed by drying to remove solvent.

Boards or planks of decking that had been removed were stacked solid in a large pile. Drying was occurring primarily on the surface of the material. Since the steamboat lies lower than the water table, it was necessary to lower the water level by a system of wells which were constantly being pumped. It is obvious that continued pumping cannot be maintained during winter months. Water will, therefore, fill the excavation during the winter and completely submerge the steamboat until pumping can again be resumed.

Submersion of the steamboat again in water will not appreciably damage the wooden structure. Repeated wetting and drying of wood will tend to increase the size of checks or cracks. However, since checking has already occurred in the surface of the wood that has been exposed to drying conditions, one additional soaking and drying period will have only a slight effect on increasing the size of the checks and the subsequent strength.

The oak beams and planking of the steamboat are quite sound. There are, however, structural weaknesses in parts of the major beams that resulted from sinking of the midsection below the level of the bow and stern. It is my opinion that damage to the boat will result if it were to be lifted above the water surface by mechanical means. It does have sufficient structural strength, however, to be readily moved in water. In other words, if the silt surrounding the boat were removed and the bottom (primarily the midsection) loosed from the clay that now binds it, the boat could, with the aid of buoys, be readily raised to water level. It has already been experienced that the bow will rise with a rise in water level. It has also been shown that most of the water soaked decking, in which no drying occurred, will float in water. Therefore, the weight to be lifted in water may only be the weight of the soil in the bottom structure of the boat and the metal fittings. Therefore, raising of the steamboat in water should cause but little strain in the structure except for that which may be exerted when the fractured beams (resulting from sinking of the middle section below the bow and stern) tends to straighten when the boat is surfaced.

RECOMMENDATIONS

It was recommended that the decking material be so stacked

that air would flow between the boards. This hastened drying of the boards and reduced decomposition. Wood containing less than 20 percent moisture will not support decay. Wood in the Nebraska area will contain considerably less than 20 percent moisture when in equilibrium with the atmosphere. Therefore, it will not be necessary to supply wood-preserving chemicals to prevent decay of this material if the material is properly dried. The top boards of the stack should be covered, as rapid drying in direct sunlight causes excessive checking.

Treatment of this checking with polyethylene glycol to reduce shrinkage was not recommended. The checks that are now on the surface of the boards would, no doubt, be partially closed by an effective treatment; however, it is my opinion that, in general, the advantages gained by polyethylene glycol would not warrant the cost.

Treatment of wood with polyethylene glycol-4000 carried out at the U.S. Forest Products Laboratory, Madison, Wis., has shown that satisfactory results can be obtained by using this chemical in an aqueous as well as an alcoholic solution. It was recommended, therefore, that tests be made to determine the suitability of water as a solvent for the polyethylene glycol-4000. Considerable savings can be made by eliminating the cost of the alcohol. It eliminates the fire hazard that exists when alcohol is present. The chief advantage of the alcohol solution appears to be the reduced time required to dry treated wood, but the cost of alcohol seems to be a high price to pay.

In using polyethylene glycol in an aqueous solution, it is still necessary to maintain the treating solution at the elevated temperature, as is done with an alcoholic solution. It is necessary to maintain this elevated temperature in order to reduce the viscosity of the polyethylene glycol-4000. The viscosity is a major factor in determining the rate of movement of the solution into the wood. At a temperature of 65° C., the viscosity of polyethylene glycol-4000 is practically the same as that of polyethylene glycol-1000 at room temperature.

The movement of solvent (either alcohol or water) from treated wood is slow. Solvent remaining in the wood after it is assumed to be dry will tend to keep the wood in a swollen state for a considerable length of time, and thus give one a false impression of the effectiveness of the treatment. It is necessary to know the efficiency of the process used in order to be certain that the wood is satisfactorily treated. It was, therefore, recommended that tests be made to determine the percent reduction in shrinkage that is imparted to wood by these treatments. By so doing, a comparison of the effectiveness of various treatments can be made. Also, the effectiveness of material already treated can be determined. In addition, by knowing the percent reduction in shrinkage that is imparted by the treatment, the minimum length of time of treatment can be determined.

It was recommended that should the steamboat be removed from the water in the future, it should, as soon as practical, be shielded from exposure to direct sunlight and from repeated wetting and drying to minimize additional surface checking.

DIMENSIONAL STABILIZATION

The degree of dimensional stabilization of wood by chemical treatment, such as with polyethylene glycol, phenolic resin, etc., depends on the amount of solids that are deposited in the cell wall structure that remains after drying. Only solids that are deposited in the cell walls of the wood reduce shrinking; that deposited in the voids is of no value. In general, the solids do not react with the wood, but only act to bulk it. The extent to which solids enter the cell walls depends on the degree to which the cell walls have been swollen. Chemicals dissolved in solvents that do not swell wood, such as benzene, cannot enter the cell walls and, therefore, will impart no dimensional stabilization. Polyethylene glycol will not diffuse into dry wood until the wood is first swollen with the solvent of the treating solution.

TREATMENT WITH PEG-1000

The treatment of wood in an aqueous solution of polyethylene glycol-1000 will impart a high degree of dimensional stabilization. This work is described in numerous articles published in technical journals. The treatment of waterlogged wood from archeological sites as a means of preservation is described in the article "Conservation of 200-year-old waterlogged boats with polyethylene glycol" by Ray M. Seborg and Robert B. Inverarity, *Studies in Conservation*, vol. 7, no. 4, November 1962.

The major disadvantage of using this chemical of lower molecular weight is that the treated wood tends to sweat or bleed at relatively high humidities. This tendency to bleed, however, can be greatly reduced by a surface coating of polyurethane finish (Tranco 542F), obtainable from Trancoa Chemical Corporation, Reading, Mass. It may be of interest to compare the percent reduction in the shrinkage of wood when treated with polyethylene glycol-1000 with that obtained for comparable wood samples treated with polyethylene glycol-4000.

CALCULATION OF SHRINKAGE

Percent reduction in shrinkage can be readily determined by cutting cross-sections from comparable samples of treated and untreated boards, and measuring changes in dimensions from wet to air-dry conditions. To obtain an average value, cross-sections 1/8-inch to 1/4-inch thick should be cut from at least five different boards. The length of the cross-sections should be approximately the same for ease of measurement. Lengths of 1- to 1 1/2-inches are quite easy to measure. The height of the sample is the board thickness. The length of the wet-untreated, and wet-treated cross-sections should be determined directly after cutting, that is, before drying of the sections occur, or stored under nondrying conditions until measurements can be made. Measurements should be made preferably with a dial gage reading to 1/1000th of an inch. The samples should then be air-dried to constant weight and again measured. Drying of the cross-sections can be accomplished quite readily if the samples are placed on a screen and air is allowed to circulate over both faces with use of a fan. The percent reduction in shrinkage due to the treatment is computed by the formula:

$$P = 1 - \frac{S_t}{S_c} \times 100$$

Where: P is the percent reduction in shrinkage; S_t is the percent shrinkage of the treated wood; S_c is the percent shrinkage of the control (untreated) wood.

When treating wet or water-soaked wood, the percent of polyethylene glycol in the solution will change because of the diffusion of water from the wood into the treating solution. It is, therefore, desirable to determine the concentration of polyethylene glycol in the solution. This can be done by determining the specific gravity of the treating solution by use of a hydrometer and then referring to the manufacturer's chart to find the percent of polyethylene glycol. Although this chart has been computed for polyethylene glycol-200, it can be used for other polyethylene glycols in aqueous solutions; the density of polyethylene glycols with molecular weights of 200, 1,000, and 4,000 are only slightly different. This chart cannot be used for determining the concentration of polyethylene glycols in an alcohol solution.

Samples of wood taken from the steamboat were submitted to Dr. B. F. Kukachka, Specialist, Wood Identification, U.S. Forest Products Laboratory, for identification of species. Samples taken from the large structural beams (cylinder timbers) and from the 2-inch-thick planking on the sides of the boat were identified as white oak. Samples taken from the bulkheads, decking, crates, and staves from a wood container were all identified as white pine.

There is generally some decay and darkening of the wood in areas around iron spikes and bolts in the oak planking and beams. This is the result of the chemical reaction that occurs between the iron and tannins and, possibly, other extractives in the wood, especially in oak. This reaction decreases as the wood is dried. This effect is, of course, of little importance in the overall problem of salvaging the boat, and nothing can be done about it. I mention it merely in event that some question is raised in future years regarding this discoloration around the metal fastenings.

In my opinion it would be desirable to retain several dried samples of each of the various wood artifacts without chemical treatment. Such samples would show the difference in the treated and untreated wood and emphasize the effectiveness of such treatments. The untreated wood should be dried slowly (not in an oven or in direct sunlight), preferably in a cool room, and stacked in order that drying occurs equally on all faces to prevent cupping. Slow drying will minimize checking of the wood.

RAISING THE BOAT

It is not within the scope of this report to advise on means of raising this steamboat. Such an undertaking, no doubt, will be carried out only after consulting with engineers and scientific personnel versed in this field of work. However, since in my opinion this steamboat would be damaged by mechanical lifting, I would like to comment favorably on the method of floating the boat to different levels in the manner in which ships are raised in canals from one level to another. The water table of the excavated pit rises to within 10 feet of the land surface. Therefore, if an adjacent excavation or ditch is made of sufficient size and depth (20 feet) to hold the boat, the water would fill the ditch to a depth of 10 feet (estimated draft of the boat). The boat could then be towed into the ditch; the end of the ditch could then be blocked by a dirt filling. This ditch would now be comparable to a "lock" in a canal. By filling this ditch with water, the boat could be again raised. If an embankment could be made around the ditch and around a ground level area, the boat could be floated into this area for permanent display. This procedure, of course, would depend on the ability of the soil to hold water. Possibly some surface coating could be sprayed on the surface of the upper levels to make it less pervious to water. If such a process proved successful, probably the only damage that would occur would be that resulting from the straightening of those parts of the beams that were bent and already somewhat damaged.

TREATMENT OF THE BOAT

The type and extent of treatment to be given to the timbers and planking in the steamboat, should it be raised in the future, is a difficult decision. Certainly, consultation should first be made with various organizations, government agencies, and individuals. One factor to be considered would be the cost of the various treatments that may be proposed and availability of funds. Another factor would be the effectiveness of such treatments, if necessary. If treatments to reduce decay are required, they can probably be made by surface coating the wood with wood-preserving chemicals. Information on types of preservatives and methods of application are available from the American Wood Preservers Association, 1012 14th Street, Washington, D.C., or from the U.S. Forest Products Laboratory, P.O. Box 5130, Madison, Wis.

Treatment to reduce further surface checking can be accomplished by the application of several surface coatings of polyethylene glycol; a small section of the bulkhead has already had one coating. Some reduction in surface checking was observed, although the effect is quite minor. To be effective, multiple coatings would have to be applied. Such coatings are chiefly effective if applied to the wood surface *before any appreciable drying of the wood surface* occurs.

Treatment to dimensionally stabilize the wood, to prevent the wood from shrinking, is difficult to achieve in beams and planking. In addition, it is especially difficult if the material cannot be immersed in the treating solution such as can be done with small artifacts. Penetration of polyethylene glycol in the outer regions of the wood structure will not significantly reduce shrinking of the beams or planking; untreated wood in the central areas will still shrink upon drying. This drying will be slow and, for the thick beams, may occur over a period of many years. It is doubtful that sufficient stabilization can be obtained by any practical treatment to prevent a major fraction of the shrinking of these thick wood structures.

Therefore, if adequate dimensional stabilization of the wood is not attained, and if the boat is not kept at high moisture levels after it is removed from the water, it can be expected that the 2-inch planks will slowly shrink, leaving cracks or gaps between the planks. These openings can be subsequently caulked if desired. The large oak beams will also shrink over a period of years, and will result in the ends of the bolts protruding above the wood. The bolts can be rethreaded and tightened. It is my opinion that such shrinkage can be accepted, and should not detract from the beauty or value of such a potentially fine museum relic.

APPENDIX C

A Study of the Volume, Weight, and Density of the Bertrand Hull

—Pamela Hengeveld

This study was undertaken to obtain a rough estimate of the total volume and weight of the emptied hull of the *Bertrand*, and to calculate density as a means of determining the degree of buoyancy of the hull as a single unit after a given length of time of exposure to the atmosphere.

METHODS AND MATERIALS

The hull, as of September, 1969, consisted solely of wooden parts and a small but not negligible quantity of metal. All cargo, decking, engine parts, and remnants of superstructure had been removed. Volume data for both wood and metal were determined by measurement of representative component parts with the use of chain and ruler to tolerances of 1/4th inch. Weights of wooden components were calculated by removing small, representative samples with a Swedish increment bore of 3/16th-inch diameter, and by a 1.1 inch drill bit. The core samples were weighed on a Mettler Analytical Balance to within 1/10,000th of a gram. Reduction of density figures in grams per cubic inch to pounds per cubic foot was accomplished with an Olivetti Programma 101 computer.[1]

Sample cores were removed from 17 representative components of the hull, each of which had been exposed to the air for approximately four and a half months. Immediately upon removal, the

---

[1]The use of the computer and analytical balance was generously offered by the Departments of Mathematics and Chemistry, Dana College, Blair, Nebr.

core samples and shavings from a drill bit sample of the bottom hull were sealed in polyethylene bags and removed to the laboratory for weighing.

The major components thus sampled include the following: a portion of an exemplary upper rudder assembly, the transom, an exemplary inner and outer cylinder timber, the keelson, an exemplary horizontal (hull floor) and vertical (hull side) rib, side bracing members, an exemplary side hull member (strake), an exemplary stanchion for cylinder supporting timber, rudder supporting beam, the hull planking, the guards, boiler supporting beams, a bottom hull member, and a bulkhead.

The remaining metal parts of the hull were entirely of wrought iron. As in the case of the wooden components, the dimensions of metal parts, with the exception of cut nails, were recorded and the computer was programmed for the standard density of wrought iron, i.e., 128.80 grams per cubic inch. An area equal to 1/80th the total area of the hull surface was marked off and all nails were removed, weighed, then replaced. The result was multiplied by 80 to compute total weight of all nails in the hull. Among the major metal parts measured—and remaining on the hull—were a capstan shaft and gear, strake bolts, nuts and washers, supporting rods and hog chains of various diameters and lengths, pillow blocks, and U-bolts, brackets, cleats, the bow ice shield, miscellaneous metal straps, and several large turnbuckles.

WOOD SAMPLE DATA

Bore A: Upper rudder assembly, (starboard side). Volume and weight data doubled to include port side. Volume: 12' 3" x 10" x 10" (x2); Weight of bore: 3.1945 gm. Bore: 3, 16" diam. x 10" length. Bore density: 11.5694 gm./cu. in. or, 43.98 lbs./cu. ft.

Bore B: Transom plank. Volume: 5" x 1' 9" x 30'; Weight of bore: 1.2332 gm. Bore: 3/16" diam. x 5" length. Bore density: 8.9325 gm./cu. in. or 33.96 lbs./cu. ft.

Bore C: Inner cylinder timber (starboard side; volume data doubled to include port side). Volume: 2' 6" x 7" x 46" (x 2); Weight of bore: 2.0719 gm. Bore: 3/16" diam. x 7" length. Bore density: 10.7196 gm./cu. in. or 40.75 lbs./cu. ft.

Bore D: Keelson. Volume: 160' x 5" x 12"; Weight of bore: 4.8580 gm. Bore: 3/16" diam. x 12" length. Bore density: 14.6647 gm./cu. in or 55.75 lbs./cu. ft.

Bore E: Ribs (vertical). Volume data multiplied by 220 to include all vertical ribs (starboard and port sides). Volume: (mean) 3" x 4" x 5' (x 220); Weight of bore: 1.3424 gm. Bore: 3/16" diam. x 4" length. Bore density: 12.1543 gm./cu. in. or 46.21 lbs./cu. ft.

Bore F: Ribs (hull floor, horizontal). Volume data multiplied by 110 to include all horizontal ribs. Volume: 3" x 6" x 30' (x 110); Weight of bore: 1.7360 gm. Bore: 3/16" diam. x 6" length. Bore density: 10.4787 gm./cu. in. or 39.84 lbs./cu. ft.

Bore G: Side bracing members, port side. Volume data doubled to include starboard side. Volume: 2" x 2' x 160' (x 2); Weight of bore: .6587 gm. Bore: 3/16" diam. x 2" length. Bore density: 11.9280 gm./cu. in. or 45.35 lbs./cu. ft.

Bore H: Side hull members, port side. Volume data doubled to include starboard side. Volume: 2" x 5' x 160' (x 2); Weight of bore: .3714 gm. Bore: 3/16" diam. x 2" length. Bore density: .3714 gm./cu. in or 25.57 lbs./cu. ft.

Bore I: Outer cylinder timber, starboard side. Volume data doubled to include port side. Volume: 6 1/4" x 2' x 23' (x 2); Weight of bore: 2.1181 gm. Bore: 3/16" diam. x 6 1/4" length. Density of bore: 12.2737 gm./cu. in. or 46.66 lbs./cu. ft.

Bore J: Port hog frame supporting beam (small keelson). Volume data doubled to include starboard side. Volume: 8" x 1' x 41' (x 2); Weight of bore: 3.3531 gm. Bore: 3/16" diam. x 8" length. Density of bore: 15.1798 gm./cu. in or 57.71 lbs./cu. ft.

Bore K: Remaining bulkhead. Volume: 1 3/4" x 2' x 160'; Weight of bore: .2023 gm. Bore: 3/16" diam. x 1 3/4" length. Density of bore: 4.1867 gm./cu. in. or 15.92 lbs./cu. ft.

Bore L: Rudder supporting beams, starboard side. Volume data doubled to include port side. Volume: 1' 6" x 8" x 5' 2" (x 2); Weight of bore: 1.8656 gm. Bore: 3/16" diam. x 6" length. Density of bore: 11.2610 gm./cu. in. or 42.81 lbs./cu. ft.

Bore M: Stanchions for cylinder supporting beams and bulkhead supporting beams. Volume: 3" x 3" x 240'; Weight of bore: .9908 gm. Bore: 3/16" diam. x 6" length. Bore density: 12.0167 gm./cu. in or 45.68 lbs./cu. ft.

Bore N: Hull planking. Volume: 2" x 23' x 320'; Weight

of bore: .8874 gm. Bore: 3/16" diam. x 3" length. Bore density: 10.7127 gm./cu. in. or 40.73 lbs./cu. ft.

Bore O: Guard: Volume : 3' 8" x 2 1/2' x 142'; Weight of bore: .9843 gm. Bore: 3/16" diam. x 3" length. Bore density 11.8827 gm./cu. in. or 45.17 lbs./cu. ft.

BoreP: Boiler supporting beams (gunwale to gunwale) Volume: 9" x 9" x 30' + 13" x 9" x 30' + 7" x 4" x 20' + 7" 4" x 14' + 7" x 4" x 8' + 7" x 4" x 9' + 6" x 10" x 10'; Weigh of bore: 1.7499 gm. Bore: 3/16" diam. x 6". Bore density 10.5626 gm./cu. in. or 40.15 lbs./cu. ft.

Bore Q: Bottom hull members. Volume: 3" x 30' x 160' Weight of bore: (mean weight of 4 sample bores) 46.859? gm. Bore: 1.1" diam. x 3" length. Bore density: 16.4363 gm. cu. in. or 62.48 lbs./cu. ft.

For purposes of calculation, the wood and metal parts were categorized by simple geometric shape. Most wooden parts were sim ple rectangular solids; therefore, the volume was determined simpl by multiplying the dimensions of length by width by thickness. The cores used to determine the density of the representative parts were cylinders whose volumes were determined by multiplying the area o the circular base by the height of the core. The computer was pro grammed to accept volume data of the metal for a variety of geo metric forms. For example, a bolt was classed as a cylinder, and it head, as a rectangular solid. The nut was classed as a rectangular solic with a cylindrical void, and a washer, or a pipe, as cylindrical solid with cylindrical voids. In the programming process, the outer dimen sions of the object was fed to the computer and, where applicable, the void to be subtracted.

RESULTS

Each sample removed from the 17 representative wooder components of the hull was found to be of a different density. The total volume of the wood was calculated at 3,888 cubic feet, and the weight at 182,795 pounds, i.e., a density of approximately 47.? pounds per cubic foot. The volume of the metal was calculated at jus short of 20 cubic feet. Using the standard figure of 128.80 grams pe cubic inch as the average density of wrought iron, the total weight o the metal was calculated at 9,837 pounds, or almost 5 tons. The tota weight of wood and metal, 192,632 pounds, divided by the total vol ume of 3,908 cubic feet, produces a figure of 49.3 pounds per cubi foot (overall density), considerably less than the density of fresh wa ter, i.e., 62.4 pounds per cubic foot.

CONCLUSIONS

Wood densities varied from sample to sample, ranging from 4.92 pounds per cubic foot, to 62.48 pounds per cubic foot. The later figure was derived from the weight and volume data taken from the slightly nonbuoyant bottom hull planks which were often awash during the months of exposure, and only the tops (or one plane surface) of which were exposed to the air at any time. This appears to substantiate the empirical judgement of the archeologist on the site who noted that the white oak objects (as opposed to those of white pine) which were removed from the water always sank when placed back unless allowed to dry for a few hours. While no study was made to determine the exact amount of time a given volume and surface of the white oak would have to be exposed before it would float, given the manner in which the boat was excavated, it would appear that buoyancy of even the most massive components would be assured in a matter of a few days exposure to the open air.

Major criticism that can be made of this study involves the number and size of the sample. While the Swedish increment bore is a reasonably accurate tool, the sample bore diameter of 3/16th inch, in view of the enormous volume of the boatwood, involves an uncomfortably great range of error.

APPENDIX D

A Study of Wood Drying Rates and Water Content in the Bertrand Hull

—Pamela Hengeveld

The major objective of this study was to obtain data on the rate at which selected wooden components were drying for a range of times of exposure to the atmosphere. The study was also designed to determine percentages of water weight in the wood at various depths from component surfaces, and to determine that ratio of water to cellulose weight which would result in buoyancy. The study was initiated in anticipation of the possibility that the boat hull might, in the future, be preserved in a dry state. Inasmuch as the long term condition of the boatwood will depend upon rates of drying and the effectiveness of temperature and humidity controls, acquisition of information regarding drying rates, where component parts were exposed to the natural, open air environment for varying periods of time, seemed advisable.

Early in the 1969 period of excavation of the *Bertrand* it was noted that surface checking of the wood occurred within a day of exposure. After several weeks, fissures as deep as 1/2 inch developed in major structural supporting components. However, the rate of

---

[1]The majority of the components tested in this study were exposed to similar weather conditions, *i.e.*, somewhat below normal temperatures and somewhat higher precipitation than in previous years for the months of May through October. Mean daily high for the period: 76.2°; mean daily low: 54.4°; deviation of precipitation from normal: +2.6 inches. Data compiled by U.S. Weather Bureau Station, Blair, Nebr.; *Climatologica Data*, vol. 74, nos. 5-10, U.S. Department of Commerce, Environmental Science Services Administration, Lincoln, Nebr.

checking of the white oak—the predominant type of wood comprising the major supporting members—appeared, on simple visual inspection, to level off after approximately six weeks exposure to the air.[1]

It was also noted that certain wooden components removed from the boat were buoyant, and others non-buoyant. Approximately 95 percent of the white pine decking, for example, floated when placed in tanks of water—most of which was exposed to the air from only one to two hours. Still others, such as fragments of white oak stanchions, sank immediately when placed in the same tanks. When exposed to the air for several hours, however, these same white oak members became buoyant.

In this study small sections of cores of wood were subjected to a simple sink-float test, and companion samples taken from very near the same point were tested in the laboratory to determine actual percentage of water by weight. By these means it was hoped that limited information might be obtained on the rate of drying at various depths from component surfaces where the elapsed time of exposure was known.

METHODS AND MATERIALS

Sample cores were obtained with a Swedish increment bore, 3/16th inch in diameter. Samples were taken of various white oak members of the boat, consideration given to obtaining samples from components varying in the amount of time their surface (or surfaces) were exposed to the air, but away from the direct rays of the sun, and representing a variety of structural shapes and sizes. The greatest exposure time represented is six months; the least, three weeks.

At each of the 11 sample points, two cores were taken approximately 1 inch apart and to the same depth, *i.e.*, to that point most distant from an exposed surface—presumably that point which would be expected to retain the greatest percentage of water. For example, in the case of the side hull, where only one plane surface was exposed to the air, the sample was taken from the exposed surface all the way through the member to the outboard surface (immediately adjacent to the wet sand). The samples from the upper rudder assembly, exposed to the air on four sides, were taken from one surface to that point most distant from the four sides.

The cores were identified with a prefix number indicating the source or point of sampling, followed either by the letter A, used to designate core sections subjected to the sink-float test, or by B, the core sections removed to the laboratory to determine water by weight. At each sample point, core A was cut in 1 centimeter sections and numbered consecutively from the exposed surface inward. Each centimeter section was immediately dropped into a glass of water to observe buoyancy. "Floaters" were recorded with the plus sign (+), and "sinkers" with a negative sign (-).

The second core, B, was taken from within an inch of core A, immediately cut into one centimeter lengths, numbered consecutively from exposed surface inward, and placed in 1 1/2-inch lengths of small plastic tubes. The ends of the sections were sealed with plastic tape to eliminate evaporation. The B core sections were taken to the laboratory where their weights were recorded to within 1/10,000th of a gram on a Mettler analytical balance. After the sections were placed in an oven for 48 hours at 110 degrees F., their weights were again recorded. Differences between their weights when wet and when dry were determined, and percentages of water by weight for sections of the B core series were computed and charted.

OVEN TIME CONTROL

Minimal oven time for the elimination of water from the B core series was determined in the following manner: A centimeter section of white oak, 3/16th inch in diameter, from the *Bertrand* with a density greater than water at room temperature (initial weight of 0.1630 gram) was placed in a small vacuum flask containing tap water. The pressure was reduced to 18 mm. with an ordinary laboratory aspirator. Following a 10 minute exposure to these conditions at a temperature of 22° C., atmospheric pressure was restored (barometer uncorrected at 726 mm. with the sample under water). The sample was permitted to remain under water for several minutes, was then removed from the flask and excess surface water was removed by gently rolling the small cylinder on paper toweling. The weight at this point was 0.1800 gram, a gain of 10.4 percent over the initial weight. During exposure to the low pressure, copious bubbling occurred at many points over the surface of the sample. This may have been due to the evolution of air from the interstices of the sample and/or various points on the surface acting as nucleii for boiling. After two additional cycles under analogous conditions, the sample weight had increased to 0.1840 gram, a gain of 12.9 percent.

At this point the sample was again placed in tap water at room temperature and pressure where it was allowed to remain for 40 hours, after which the sample weighed 0.1898 gram. Processing through an additional aqueous vacuum cycle reduced the weight to 0.1879 gram. Replacing the sample in water at room temperature and pressure for eight hours increased its weight to 0.1897 gram. Drying the sample in an oven at 110° C. for 18 hours reduced its weight to 0.0960 gram, a decrease of 49.4 percent of its maximum net weight.

After an additional oven drying period of 30 hours, the sample weight was recorded at 0.0954 gram. Exposure of the sample to dry vacuum conditions for 22 hours (25° C. at 6 mm. pressure) did not significantly affect its weight (0.0959 gram). Based on these observations, it seems reasonable to conclude that the maximum amount of water that the white oak members of the *Bertrand* can contain (absorbed and interstitial water) approximates 98 percent of its dry weight.[2]

DATA SUMMARY

The results of the A and B core series appear below and in graphs 1 through 11 (fig. 97).

Cores 1-A, 1-B: Location: upper portion of starboard rudder assembly; exposure time: six months; material: white oak. Core series A(+): float; (-): sink. Percentages of water by weight given for sections of B core series. Centimeter sections 1 (outside) through 13 (inside): 1.+, 12.1; 2.+, 16.0; 3.+, 22.3; 4.+, 37.6; 5.+, 33.8; 6.+, 35.5; 7.+, 36.6; 8.+, 40.4; 9.-, 41.4; 10.-, 39.9; 11.-, 40.6; 12.-, 45.6; 13.-, 48.0.

Cores 2-A, 2-B: Location: lower portion of starboard rudder assembly; exposure time: three months; material: white oak. Core series A (+): float; (-): sink. Percentages of water by weight given for sections of core series B. Centimeter sections 1 (outside) through 13 (inside): 1.+, 12.6; 2.+, 20.8; 3.+, 31.7; 4.+, 36.7; 5.-, 42.3; 6.-, 46.0; 7.-, 44.8; 8.-, 46.5; 9.-, 45.8; 10.-, 45.8; 11.-, 47.4; 12.-, 44.8; 13.-, 40.7.

Cores 3-A, 3-B: Location: rib, port side, midship; exposure time: three weeks; material: white oak. Core series A(+): float; (-): sink. Percentages of water by weight given for sections of core series B. Centimeter sections 1 (outside) through 10 (inside): 1.-, 48.1; 2.-, 51.3; 3.-, 49.7; 4.-, 48.5; 5.-, 47.3; 6.-, 47.6; 7.-, 47.3; 8.-, 48.6; 9.-, 48.4; 10.-, 47.8.

Cores 4-A, 4-B: Location: forward longitudinal center brace; exposure time: three and one-half months; material: white oak. Core series A(+): float; (-): sink. Percentages of water by weight given for sections of core series B. Centimeter sections 1 (outside) through 10 (inside): 1.+, 19.6; 2.+, 30.0; 3.+, 33.7; 4.+, 35.9; 5.+, 38.0; 6.+, 40.6; 7.+, 39.9; 8.+, 37.8; 9.-, 34.8; 10.-, 36.7.

[2]The portion of this study directed to the determination of minimal oven time for the elimination of water in the B core series was conducted by Frank Hengeveld, Chairman, Department of Chemistry, Dana College, Blair, Nebr.

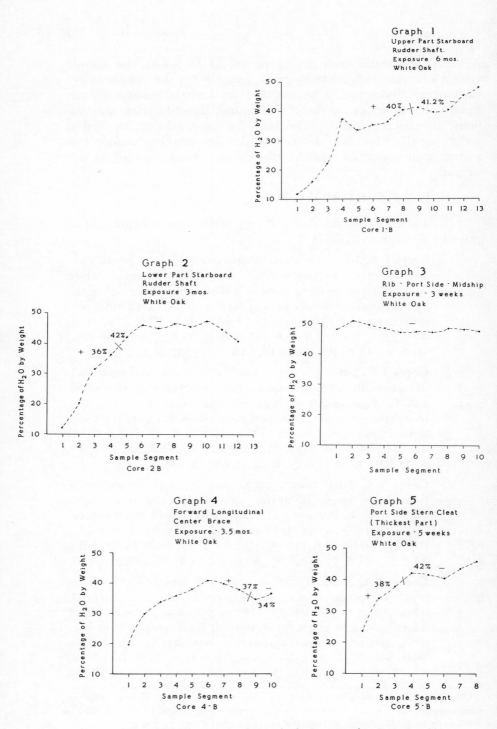

Figure 97. Percentage of water in the B core series, Cores 1 to 11.

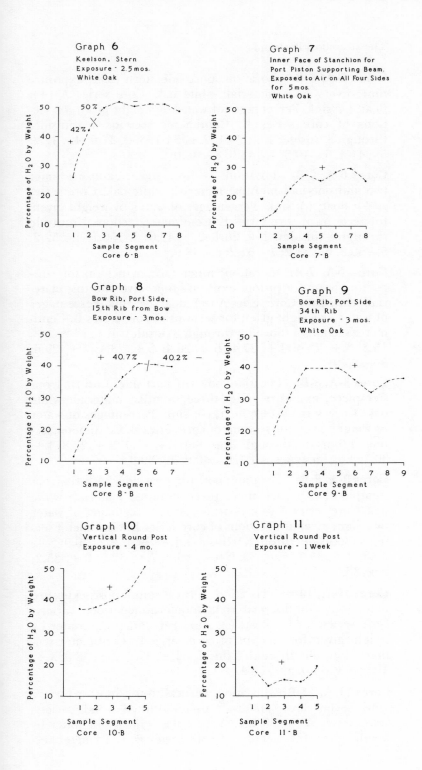

Graph 6

Keelson, Stern
Exposure - 2.5 mos.
White Oak

Core 6-B

Graph 7

Inner Face of Stanchion for
Port Piston Supporting Beam.
Exposed to Air on All Four Sides
for 5 mos.
White Oak

Core 7-B

Graph 8

Bow Rib, Port Side,
15th Rib from Bow
Exposure - 3 mos.

Core 8-B

Graph 9

Bow Rib, Port Side
34th Rib
Exposure - 3 mos.
White Oak

Core 9-B

Graph 10

Vertical Round Post
Exposure - 4 mo.

Core 10-B

Graph 11

Vertical Round Post
Exposure - 1 Week

Core 11-B

Cores 5-A, 5-B: Location: port side stern cleat; exposure time: five weeks; material: white oak. Core series A (+): float; (-): sink. Percentages of water by weight given for sections of core series B. Centimeter sections 1 (outside) through 8 (inside: 1.+, 23.4; 2.+, 34.1; 3.+, 37.6; 4.-, 42.2; 5.-, 41.4; 6.-, 40.6; 7.-, 43.6; 8.-, 46.0.

Cores 6-A, 6-B: Location: keelson, stern; exposure time: two and one-half months; material; white oak. Core series A(+): float; (-): sink. Percentages of water by weight given for sections of core series B. Centimeter sections 1 (outside through 8 (inside): 1.+, 26.1; 2.+, 42.0; 3.-, 50.1; 4.-, 52.2; 5.-, 50.8; 6.-, 51.2; 7.-, 51.2; 8.-, 48.9.

Cores 7-A, 7-B: Location; inner face, stanchion for supporting beam for piston; exposure time: five months; material: white oak. Core series A (+): float; (-): sink. Percentages of water by weight given for sections of core series B. Centimeter sections 1 (outside) through 8 (inside): 1.+, 12.2; 2.+, 15.3; 3.+, 23.0; 4.+, 27.4; 5.+, 26.4; 6.+, 28.4; 7.+, 29.6; 8.+, 25.9.

Cores 8-A, 8-B: Location: bow rib, port side, 15th rib from stempiece; exposure time: three months; material: white oak. Core series A(+); float; (-): sink. Percentages of water by weight given for sections of core series B. Centimeter sections 1 (outside) through 7 (inside):1.+, 11.4; 2.+, 22.8; 3.+, 30.7; 4.+, 36.4; 5.+, 40.7; 6.-, 40.2; 7.-, 39.9.

Cores 9-A, 9-B: Location: bow rib, port side, 34th rib from stempiece; exposure time: three months; material: white oak. Core series A (+): float; (-): sink. Percentages of water by weight given for sections of core series B. Centimeter sections 1 (outside) through 9 (inside):1.+, 19.4; 2.+, 30.9; 3.+, 39.3; 4.+, 39.7; 5.+, 39.7; 6.+, 36.0; 7.+, 32.2; 8.+, 35.2; 9.+, 36.5.

Cores 10-A, 10-B: Location: vertical round post; exposure time: four months; material: undetermined wood variety. Core series A (+): float; (-): sink. Percentages of water by weight given for sections of core series B. Centimeter sections 1 (outside) through 5 (inside):1.+, 37.7; 2.+, 38.0; 3.+, 40.0; 4.+, 43.0; 5.+, 50.4.

Cores 11-A, 11-B: Location: vertical round post; exposure time: seven days; material: undetermined wood variety. Core Series A (+): float; (-): sink. Percentages of water by weight given for sections of core series B. Centimeter sections 1 (outside) through 5 (inside):1.+, 19.0; 2.+, 13.1; 3.+, 15.1; 4.+, 14.5; 5.+, 19.3.

RESULTS

The results of the sink-float test (A core series) were reasonably consistent. In each case the sections either sank or floated; none appeared to suspend in water. Three types of cores were noted, those in which all sections floated, those in which all sections sank, and those in which one or more of the outside sections floated, followed by those which sank. In only one case was a sequence noted in which some segments floated, followed by some that sank, followed by inside sections that floated. It was subsequently discovered that this core was taken from a component which had cracked, resulting in an additional drying surface and a core dryer on both ends than in the middle. This core was discarded, and another taken from a neighboring rib.

Percentages of water by weight in the B core series ranged from about 11 to over 50 percent. In cores 1-B, 2-B, and 4-B through 10-B, the water content was lower at the outside surface, and rose gradually in successively deeper centimeter segments. Core 3-B was taken from a rib that had been exposed for three weeks, but which had been submerged each day for several hours, a result of the failure of the well point system to bring the water table completely below the hull bottom. In this case, the wood remained very wet throughout, the percentage of water falling near the 50 percent line. Cores 10-B and 11-B (graphs 10,11) were taken from a vertical round post near the keelson approximately 35 feet to the rear of the bow. The type of wood is not identified, although from casual inspection it is strikingly unlike the white oak, being much softer and lighter in weight. These two cores and 3-B (the sample from the rib subjected to daily submergence) are eliminated in mean calculations of water by weight and exposure times in this study.

The transition of buoyancy to non-buoyancy appears remarkably consistent, i.e., at approximately 40 percent of water by weight. The average maximum percentage of water by weight for which a centimeter section remains buoyant is calculated at 39.0 percent; the average lowest percentage of water by weight resulting in a non-buoyant section of core is 41.5 percent. To clarify the general trend apparent in graph 12 in which all cores are plotted (fig. 98), the water content figures were averaged for graph 13 (fig. 99). Cores 3-B, 10-B, and 11-B were eliminated for reasons cited above. All first centimeter section percentages were averaged, all second centimeter sections were averaged, etc. This graph indicates that the drying occurs, on the average, quite rapidly in the first four sections, but levels off quite sharply thereafter to approximately 40 percent water by weight. The mean exposure time of the cores represented on this graph is 3.4 months.

CONCLUSIONS

While this study of wood drying rates and water content must be considered rudimentary, two general conclusions appear warranted: 1) that the rate of drying of the remaining major structural members of the *Bertrand* will reduce sharply after an exposure of from three to six months of average summer and fall, open-air atmospheric conditions at DeSoto Bend; and, 2) that buoyancy of these same major structural members of white oak can be expected by reducing the water by weight to 39.0 percent. The feasibility of allowing the hull to dry unprotected and in the open air at the site appears quite questionable if the optimum conditions of reducing water by weight to 20 percent to minimize activity of fungi and bacteria is desired. Even should the boat eventually be exposed to the air on all sides, a substantial percentage of the volume of certain major supporting members such as keelsons and hull bottom (without some attempt at increasing the rate of drying) will remain heavily saturated with water and a target for bacteria for years.

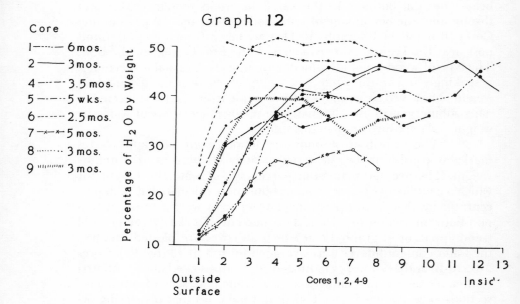

Figure 98. Percentage of water in the B core series, Cores 1, 2, 4-9.

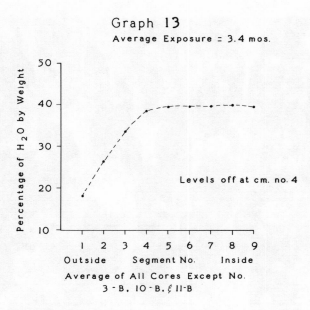

Graph 13
Average Exposure = 3.4 mos.
Percentage of H_2O by Weight
50
40
30
20
10
Levels off at cm. no. 4
1 2 3 4 5 6 7 8 9
Outside
Segment No.
Inside
Average of All Cores Except No.
3-B, 10-B, & 11-B

Figure 99. Percentage of water, B core series; average of all cores with the exception of numbers 3, 10, and 11.

Figure 100. A representative sample of the many glass and ceramic containers recovered from the holds. All glass bottles are either of the free-blown or blown-in-mold variety.

Figure 101. More than 3,000 leather boots and shoes in the cargo of the *Bertrand* were retanned in the laboratory at the DeSoto National Wildlife Refuge.

BIBLIOGRAPHY

BOOKS AND PERIODICALS

Aitken, M. J.
1961   *Physics and Archaeology.* Interscience Publishers. New York.

Alldred, J. C.
1964   "A Fluxgate Gradiometer for Archaeological Surveying," *Archaeometry,* vol. 7. Cambridge University Press. London.

Anon.
1876   "Steamboat Arrivals at Fort Benton, Montana, and Vicinity," *Contributions to the Historical Society of Montana,* vol. 1, Rocky Mountain Publishing Co. Helena.

Armitage, George T.
1961   "Prelude to the Last Roundup: the Dying Days of the Great 79," *Montana,* vol. 11, no. 4. Historical Society of Montana. Helena.

Aitkins, C. J., ed.
1908   "Log of the Steamer Robert Campbell Jr., from St. Louis to Fort Benton, Montana Territory," *Collections of the State Historical Society of North Dakota,* vol. 11. Bismarck.

Barsness, Larry
1962   *Gold Camp.* Hastings House. New York.

Bates, Alan L.
1968   *The Western Rivers Steamboat Cyclopoedium.* Hustle Press. Leonia, N. J.

Briggs, Harold E.
1929   "Pioneer River Transportation in Dakota," *North Dakota Historical Quarterly,* vol. III. Bismarck.

Burlingame, Merrill G.
1938   *The Military-Indian Frontier in Montana 1860-1890.* Iowa City, Ia.

Carr, Daniel M., ed.
1903   *Men and Women of Nebraska.* Progress Publishing Co. Fremont, Nebr.

Chapell, Phillip E.
1906   "Missouri River Steamboats," *Transactions of the Kansas State Historical Society*, vol. IX. Topeka.

Chittenden, Hiram M.
1906   "The Ancient Town of Fort Benton in Montana," *Magazine of American History*, vol. XXIV. A. S. Barnes and Co. New York.
1897   "Appendix W. W., Annual Report of the Missouri River Commission for the Fiscal Year Ending June 30, 1897, *Annual Reports of the War Department for the Fiscal Year Ended June 30, 1897*. Washington, D.C.
1903   *Life and Adventures of Joseph LaBarge*. Ross and Haines Co. Minneapolis.

Coleman, John R.
Ms.   "The Worden and Company Papers: 1860 to 1886." Manuscript, Montana State Historical Society. Helena.

Coues, Elliott, ed.
1962   *Forty Years a Fur Trader on the Upper Missouri, the Personal Narrative of Charles Larpenteur, 1833-1872*. 2 vols. Minneapolis.

Dayton, Fred E.
1925   "Steamboat days," *Nebraska History Magazine*, vol. 8. Nebraska State Historical Society. Lincoln.

Deatherage, Charles P.
1924   *Steamboating on the Missouri in the Sixties*. Priv. Pub. Kansas City, Mo.

Donovan, Frank
1966   *River Boats of America*. Thomas Y. Crowell Co. New York.

Drago, Harry Sinclair
1967   *The Steamboaters: From the Early Side-Wheelers to the Big Packets*. Dodd, Mead and Co. New York.

Editors
1885   *History of Montana, 1739-1885*. Warner Beers and Co. Helena.

Edwards, Richard and M. Hopewell
1860   *Edward's Great West and Commercial Metropolis*. St. Louis

Flectcher, Robert H.
1961   "The Day of the Cattleman Dawned Early, "*Montana*, vol. 11, no. 4. Historical Society of Montana. Helena.

Hall, Henry
1884   "Shipbuilding Industry in the United States," *Tenth Census of the United States, 1880*, vol. VIII. Washington, D.C.

Hamilton, Jean Tyree
1972   *Abel J. Vanmeter, His Park and His Diary*. Friends of Arrow Rock, Inc. Marshall, Mo.

Hodge, Paul R.
1840   *The Steam Engine, Its Origin and Gradual Improvement.* New York.

Hunter, Lewis C.
1949   *Steamboats on the Western Rivers: An Economic and Technological History.* Harvard University Press. Cambridge.

Kane, Lucile M.
1951   *Military Life in Dakota: the Journal of Phillippe Regis de-Trobriand.* St. Paul.

King, William H.
1863   *Lessons and Practical Notes on Steam, the Steam Engine, and Propellors.* 4th ed. New York.

Lass, William E.
1962   *A History of Steamboating on the Upper Missouri.* University of Nebraska Press. Lincoln.

Lyman, John
1945   "Register Tonnage and Its Measurement," The *American Neptune.* vol. 5. Mystic, Conn.

Lytle, William M.
1952   *Merchant Steam Vessels of the United States, 1807-1868.* (The Lytle List) Mystic, Conn.

May, Earl Chapin
1945   *Principio to Wheeling, 1715-1945, a Pageant of Iron and Steel.* Harper and Brothers. New York.

McBride, Fanny Fern
Ms   "Steamboating on the "Upper Missouri," MA thesis (1929) on file: University of Nebraska Library. Lincoln.

McDonald, W. J.
1927   "The Missouri River and Its Victims," *Missouri Historical Review,* vol. XXI, no. 2. State Historical Society of Missouri. Columbia.

Moss, James E., ed.
1963   "Ho! For the Gold Mines of Montana, Up the Missouri in 1865. The Journal of William H. Gallaher," *Missouri Historical Review,* vol. 57, no. 2. State Historical Society of Missouri. Columbia.

Myers, Denys P.
1952   "The Architectural Development of the Western Floating Palace," *Journal of the Society of Architectural Historians,* vol. XI, no. 4. New York.

Newton, J. H., ed.
1879   *History of the Pan Handle, West Virginia.* Wheeling, W. Va.

Parsoll, Albert J.
1949   "Frank L. Worden, Pioneer Merchant, 1830-1887," *Pacific Northwest Quarterly,* vol. 40. University of Washington. Seattle.

Petersen, William J.
1937   *Steamboating on the Upper Mississippi, the Waterway* ▮
Iowa. Iowa City.
1955   "Steamboating on the Missouri River," *Iowa Journal of H*▮
tory, vol. 53, no. 2. State Historical Society of Iowa. Iow▮
City.

Petsche, Jerome E.
1970   "Uncovering the Steamboat Bertrand," *Nebraska Histor*▮
vol. 51, no. 1. Nebraska State Historical Society. Lincoln.

Phillips, Paul C., ed.
1957   *Forty Years on the Frontier as Seen in the Journals a*▮
Reminiscences of Granville Stuart. 2 vols. Glendale.

Russell, John S.
1841   *Treatise on the Steam Engine.* London.

Russell, Norman
1861   "On American River Steamers," *Transactions of the Instit*▮
tion of Naval Architects, vol. II. London.

Sanders, Wilbur F.
1896   "Francis Lyman Worden," *Contributions to the Historic*▮
Society of Montana; with its Transactions, Act of Incorpo▮
tion, Constitution, Ordinances, vol. 2. State Publishi▮
Company. Helena.

Sheldon, Addison E., ed.
1927   *Nebraska History Magazine* (Missouri River Number), v▮
VIII, no. 1. Nebraska State Historical Society. Lincoln.

Stout, Tom
1921   *Montana, Its Story and Biography; A History of Aborigin*▮
and Territorial Montana and Three Decades of Statehoo▮
3 vols. The American Historical Society. Chicago and Ne▮
York.

Sunder, John E.
1965   *The Fur Trade on the Upper Missouri.* University of Okl▮
homa Press. Norman.

Sweeney, John M.
1888   "River Practice of the West," *Transactions of the America*▮
Society of Mechanical Engineers. vol. IX. J. J. Little and C▮
New York.
1894   "The Construction of Steamboats Navigating the Wester▮
Waters of the United States," *Proceedings of the Intern*▮
tional Engineering Congress, vol. II. New York.

Switzer, Ronald R.
1971   "Charles Parker's Britannia on the Steamboat Bertrand▮
The Museum of the Fur Trade Quarterly, vol. 7, no. ▮
Chadron, Nebr.
1970   "Lead Bars from the St. Louis Shot Tower," *The Museum* ▮
the Fur Trade Quarterly, vol. 6, no. 4, Chadron, Nebr.

1972   "Tally Ho's from the Steamboat Bertrand," *Just Buttons*, vol. 30, no. 4. Southington, Conn.

1974   "The Bertrand Bottles: A Study of 19th-Century Glass and Ceramic Containers." National Park Service, Washington, D.C.

Ms.   "Maynard Cartridges and Primers from the Steamboat Bertrand," forthcoming in: *Archaeology*. New Brunswick, N.J.

Ms.   "Civil War Howitzer Ammuniton from the Steamboat Bertrand," forthcoming in: *Archaeology*. New Brunswick, N.J.

Tredgold, Thomas
1851   *The Principles and Practice and Explanation of the Machinery Used in Steam Navigation*. London.

U.S. Department of Commerce
1969   *Climatological Data*. vol. 74, nos. 5-10. Environmental Science Services Administration, University of Nebraska. Lincoln.

Wallace, John
1865   *The Practical Engineer, Showing the Best and Most Economical Mode of Modeling, Constructing, and Working Steam Engines*. Pittsburg.

Way, Frederick Jr.
1964   *Way's Steamboat Directory* (Abridged Pocket Edition). Priv. Pub. Sewickley, Pa.

1950   *Way's Directory of Western Rivers Packets*. Priv. Pub. Sewickley, Pa.

White, Helen M., ed.
1966   *Ho! For the Gold Fields; Northern Overland Wagon Trains of the 1860s*. Minnesota State Historical Society. St. Paul.

Zacharchuk, Walter and John H. Rick
1969   "The Mallorytown Wreck," *Historical Archaeology*, vol. III. Bethlehem, Pa.

PUBLIC DOCUMENTS

Eads and Nelson vs. the Steamboat H. D. Bacon (1 Newberry 280) 1857. New York.

Herndon House Register. Microfilm, archives of the Nebraska State Historical Society. Lincoln.

Order of Reference of the Supreme Court in the Wheeling Bridge Case, 1851. Saratoga Springs, N.Y.

Record Group 36, Bureau of Customs, Federal Records Center, General Services Administration. Kansas City, Mo.

Record Group 41, Records of the Bureau of Marine Inspection and Navigation, General Services Administration, National Archives and Record Service, Washington, D.C.

Senate Executive Document No. 42, 32nd Congress, I Session Washington, D.C.

NEWSPAPERS

Cincinnati Gazette, Cincinnati, Ohio. Nov. 20, 1855; Apr. 11, 1868 and Sept. 30, 1879.

Council Bluffs Non Pareil, Council Bluffs, Iowa. Apr. 3, 1865.

Daily Missouri Democrat, St. Louis, Mo. Mar. 10 and 17; and Apr 4, 1865.

Daily Missouri Republican, St. Louis, Mo. Mar. 18; and Apr. 4 1865.

Davenport Gazette, Davenport, Iowa. Apr. 13, 1865.

Montana Post, Virginia City, Mont. Mar. 25; Apr. 1, 22, and 23 1865.

Nebraska Advertiser, Brownsville, Nebr. May 11, 1865.

Omaha Nebraskian, Omaha, Nebr. Apr. 6, 1865.

Omaha Weekly Bee, Omaha, Nebr. July 22, 1896.

Sunday Journal and Star, Lincoln, Nebr. Apr. 12, 1936.

Tri-Weekly Missouri Democrat, St. Louis, Mo. Feb. 22, Mar. 20 and Apr. 16, 1865.

Wheeling Daily Intelligencer, Wheeling, W. Va. Nov. 24 and 26 1864.

INDEX

Hardware, needs on frontier, 123-
124; in cargo: axes and parts, 69;
lead bar stock, 70; mauls, 70;
nails, 70; steel bar stock, 71; tar
paper, 71; tools, 69-70; white
lead, 70
Hatches, 34, 77
Hats. See Textiles
Hattie May (steamboat), 118
H. D. Bacon (steamboat), 102-n
Helena, Mont. Terr., 16, 125
Hell Gate, Mont. Terr., 12, 13, 123
Hengeveld, Frank, 157-n
Hengeveld, Pamela, 149, 154
Herndon House, Omaha, Nebr., 10,
124-125
Higgins, Christopher P., 12
Highley, Terry, 142
Historic Sites Act of 1935, 2
Hog chains: reconstruction, 75, 84;
turnbuckles, 85; trussing system,
79, 84; use on river boats, 81; volume, 151
Hollingsworth, F., 17-n, 24
Household goods (cargo): brooms,
63; candles, 63; candle molds, 63;
clocks and parts, 64; combs, 64;
cooking utensils, 64; churns, 65;
dye, 65; eating utensils and dishes, 65, 67; ink, 65; lamps and
parts, 66; matches, 66; mirrors,
66; soap, 67; starch, 67; stoves
and parts, 67; washboards and
tubs, 67; writing supplies, 68
Howitzer ammunition, 71, 77
Hull: bustles, 102-104; components,
75-76, 78-79, 80, 150-152; condition, 150-152; condition, 105-110;
conformity, 105; construction,
76-78; depth of hold, 77; drying
rates, 154-163; evolution in western steamboats, 101-107; interior
side views, 106; measurement of
parts, 150-152; preservation, 148;
view of bottom, 109; volume,
weight and density, 149-153
Hydrogen peroxide, in preservation, 138

Independence (steamboat), 115
Insurance of steamboats on western
rivers, 95, 121
Insurors: of *Bertrand*, 37, 126-127;

recover mercury, 126; use of divers, 37, 102, 107. See also Salvors
Inverarity, Robert B., 145
Ironstone, cargo, 64; preservation,
138

John J. Roe and Co., 17

Kanawha River, 95-n
Kate Kearney (steamboat), 118
Keelson: drying rates, 160; volume
and measurement, 150. See also
Hull
Kevels, 79
Key West (steamboat), 115
Kingman and Co., 12
Kukachka, B.F., 146

LaBarge, Joseph, 116
Labels: reconstructions, 54-55, 66;
preservation, 137
Laboratory, preservation, 130-132
Laing, George, 6
Larpenteur, Charles, 117
Last Chance. See Helena
Lead. See Metals
Leather, preservation, 139
Lewis, Clifford M., 6-n
Lida Norvell (steamboat), 88-89
Lillie Martin (steamboat), 118
Lincoln, Abraham, 126
Liquor (cargo): ale, 50; Brandy
Cock-Tail, 51; Bourbon Whiskey
Cock-Tail, 51; champagne, 59-60;
Gin Cock-Tail, 53; schnapps, 58;
wine, 59-60. See also Bitters
Logan, Wilfred D., 3, 142
Long, Stephen H., 115
Los Alamos Scientific Laboratories,
140

McNeely, F.M., 17, 24-25
McNeely party, 125
Macomb, John N., 21, 22, 24
Madison, B.F., 17-n, 24˙
Magnetometer: salvors' use at *Ber-
trand* site, 1, 28-29; surface read-
outs, 29; in archeological surveys,
28
Marias River, 117
Markel, Jacob E., 24, 26
May, Earl Chapin, 85

☆ U.S. GOVERNMENT PRINTING OFFICE : 1975 O—567-106